Chainsaw Lumbermaking

Chainsaw Lumbermaking

Will Malloff

The Taunton Press

**Cover photos and text photos
by Beth Erickson.**

First printing: June 1982
International Standard Book Number 0-918804-12-4
Library of Congress Catalog Card Number 82-80556
Printed in the United States of America

A Fine Woodworking Book

Fine Woodworking® is a trademark of The Taunton Press, Inc.,
registered in the U.S. Patent and Trademark Office.

The Taunton Press, Inc.
52 Church Hill Road
Box 355
Newtown, Connecticut 06470

Contents

IN THE FIELD

SPECIALTY MILLING

Preface

I started chainsaw lumbermaking in a serious way more than twenty years ago. I was never satisfied with the efficiency of the equipment and systems available, and so began to design and construct my own. Over the years, I've developed and refined several mills and saw chains, and now I feel I have the most effective, simplest system for ecological lumber production. To my surprise, a lot of people agree with me. The result is that everywhere I go, and no matter where I retreat, people want to talk about chainsaw lumbermaking. It's hard to explain by drawing on a napkin or in the sawdust with a stick, so when Beth Erickson agreed to work with me, I saw that a book would be the perfect way to give chainsaw lumbermaking to the world. I am especially grateful to Beth for helping with the writing and for taking the photographs. I also appreciate the help and support of my precious friends and dear family, and to my loving parents, John and Mabel Malloff, I dedicate this book.

Will Malloff

Lethbridge, Alberta
Canada 1982

IN THE SHOP

Chapter 1

Basic Lumbermaking

Anyone can make lumber. The process can be as simple or as refined as you wish to make it. In its crudest form, lumbermaking can be as uncomplicated as it looks in these photos. All you need is a chainsaw attached to a mill, a straight board, a hammer and three nails (1). The board, positioned (2) and nailed to a log (3), is a guide for the mill, which is adjusted to the depth of cut plus board thickness (4). The mill is pushed along the board (5) and the sawbar pivoted out of the log at the end of the cut (6). The board and slab are removed, the mill is adjusted for the next cut, and milling continues until the work is done (7). That's all there is to it.

But for efficient lumbermaking and the best results, there are a number of other considerations, and over the years I have found many ways to refine the basic techniques. Let's have a look at the complete process—from the saw engine, ripping chain and mill to felling trees, milling boards and specialty cuts.

1

2

3

4

6

5

7

Chapter 2

The Saw Engine

A chainsaw is designed to crosscut, in other words, to cut across the grain. To rip lumber, however, the chainsaw must cut into the end grain, parallel to the fibers of the tree. To demonstrate the difference, take a short piece of lumber and make two parallel cuts across the grain with a handsaw. Then take a chisel and remove the wood between the two cuts. Notice how easily the wood falls out when crosscut. Now repeat the process on the *end* of the piece, going with the grain. In ripping, every fiber must be cut before the wood can be removed.

In crosscutting, the demand for engine power is intermittent. The outside edges of the kerf are cut with the sides of the cutters, and the remainder of the kerf wood is easily removed by the tops of the cutters. Ripping requires at least three times as much engine power as crosscutting because the saw has to run wide open from the start to the finish of each cut. Partial power is only necessary when starting and finishing a cut; otherwise the engine has to run wide open or not at all. So when choosing a saw for lumbermaking, look for one that can deliver maximum sustained power.

I recommend a saw engine with a long piston stroke that works in the 6,000 RPM range, with a chain speed of around 3,000 feet per minute. (A long piston stroke is simply one that is equal to or longer than the diameter of the piston.) My choice of engine is the direct-drive Stihl 090. The direct-drive, automatic-clutch system delivers the speed of the engine directly to the sprocket, which is the gear that delivers power to the chain. In my opinion, this is the simplest, most reliable transmission system for lumbermaking. While the gear-reduction system on gear-drive saws is good for milling, especially for milling big wood, there can be problems. The design of a gear-drive engine is such that the transmission system is upside down during milling, which can cause a lack of lubrication that often shortens transmission life.

When I choose a saw, I do not consider fuel consumption, noise, handling, vibration or weight. Nor do I necessarily use the bar, chain and sprocket that come as standard equipment—there are often better components available from manufacturers who specialize in these accessories.

Engine Maintenance

Proper engine care is crucial to good chainsaw performance—carelessness will lead to problems. Establish a practical maintenance routine and stick to it. Constant engine surveillance will soon become second nature.

Maintenance should start with a thorough knowledge of your saw. Study your operator's manual and follow its maintenance recommendations. If your manual doesn't contain a full parts list, make sure the dealer supplies you with one.

Carburetor—A carburetor contains fuel-filter screens, choke, throttle, idle-adjustment screw, and high-speed and low-speed jets, which regulate the proportion of fuel and air. Most carburetors are set at the factory for average elevation and atmospheric pressure, so you may need to adjust the carburetor to your location. Use your manual to learn how.

Because ripping requires continuous power, I run my engine at a richer setting on the high-speed jet than recommended by the manufacturer. In crosscutting, this would cause heavy carbon deposits on the spark plug and exhaust ports; in ripping, the extra fuel that passes through the engine gives additional lubrication and prolongs engine life.

To adjust the carburetor for ripping, start the engine (with bar and chain on) with the carburetor set at the manufacturer's recommended setting. Gently warm up the engine and start a cut into a log to bring the saw up to normal operating temperature. (Always make carburetor adjustments while the engine is hot.) Open the throttle wide and unscrew the high-speed jet until the engine starts to falter and perhaps even smokes a little. Then release the throttle to the idle position and adjust the low-speed jet until you get smooth and steady acceleration up to high speed. Adjust the idle-adjustment screw so the chain doesn't run while the saw is idling. I find opening the high-speed jet ⅛ or ¼ turn more than the manufacturer recommends is quite satisfactory, but running your saw like this could affect the validity of its warranty.

Periodically check the spark plug for carbon deposits. Too much carbon means your engine is running too rich. If this is the case, reset the high-speed jet closer to the manufacturer's recommended setting. Never set the high-speed jet to a lower setting than is recommended, because too low a setting can ruin your saw in just a few seconds.

Torquing—Vibration is an inherent problem of chainsaws, and over the years I have noticed the struggle of manufacturers to design bolts, nuts and screws that won't shake loose. While modern design has come close to finding the proper bolt, nut, washer and lock nut combinations, proper torquing is still vital.

After the first few hours of operating a new engine, I torque down the head bolts to compensate for the shrinkage of the cylinder gaskets (1). Heads and cylinders are usually a one-piece unit. If you have a two-piece unit, torque both the head and the cylinder. Also torque the carburetor-mounting gasket and muffler gasket along with any loose nuts, bolts or screws. After one or two torques, most saws usually need no further torquing, but inspect yours periodically.

I lubricate often-used screws, nuts and bolts with Never-Seez, a thread-lubricating grease, but a mixture of graphite and grease also works well. On bolts, nuts and screws that loosen, I use a bolt-and-thread locking mixture called Loctite. Use this after using the cleanser sold as a companion product. Always start nuts, bolts and screws with finger pressure to help avoid crossthreading.

Air filter—The air filter of a chainsaw must thoroughly clean the air going into the carburetor. Sawdust and debris entering with the air could cause the engine bearings or pistons to seize, ruining the engine. There are three basic types of filters: wire screen, flocked screen and foam. Ripping produces finer sawdust than crosscutting, and you should keep this in mind when selecting a filter. Wire-screen filters don't stop the finer sawdust, so I prefer flocked or foam ones.

Check filters after every two or three refuelings, more frequently if working with soft woods such as cedar, or abrasive woods such as mesquite. Before removing the filter cover, brush away sawdust and debris. When a filter shows the slightest sign of clogging, you should change it (2). A fouled filter reduces engine power and increases fuel consumption by changing the proportion of air to fuel. If you notice you're using more fuel than usual, check your air filter.

Clean dirty filters in a gasoline bath or with detergent and water, and allow them to air-dry. Do not use compressed air for cleaning flocked filters because the air blows the flocking out of the screen base. I usually take several clean filters (stored in plastic bags) into the field to save myself the bother of in-the-field cleaning.

Spark plugs—Spark plugs burn out more frequently in ripping than in crosscutting. Loss of power and hard starting are often signals of a faulty spark plug. The amount of carbon, its color and the color of the spark can also indicate engine problems. Charts that identify spark plug problems are handy tools, and are available from most saw dealers and plug manufacturers.

A fairly clean electrode area and a fat, blue spark are pretty good signs of a properly functioning engine. But I have found that even a good-looking plug can be faulty, becoming a problem only under compression, when the engine is hot.

1

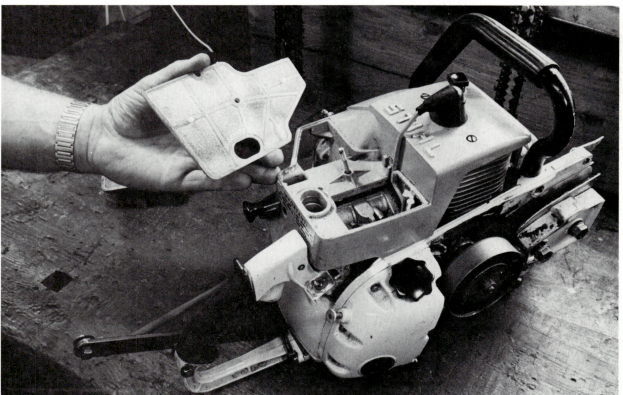

2

The Saw

To remove a spark plug, it's safer to use a rubber-cushioned spark-plug socket **(1)** rather than the T-handled combination bar and plug wrench that usually comes with chainsaws. Loosen the plug just enough to enable you to remove it by hand. If you use a wrench during the last turns, you could damage the threads.

To change plugs, remove the new plug from its container carefully and check the gap with feeler gauges or a spark-plug tool. Always use the plug recommended by the manufacturer. The length of the plug threads is precise, and using the wrong one could result in plug-to-piston contact, which would damage both components. The wrong plug can also generate too much (or too little) heat, resulting in a burnt-out piston or head, or incomplete fuel combustion.

Lubricate the plug threads **(2)** to avoid thread wear and to aid in future removal. Start the plug into the head gently, then torque with a socket. If the plug doesn't start into the head easily, inspect the head for damaged threads.

Check and service the spark plug on your saw regularly, and always have one or two extra handy in the field.

Sprockets—The sprocket drives the chain. There are two basic types available: a rim sprocket **(3)** and a spur sprocket **(4)**. The rim sprocket stands up to milling best and is the one I prefer.

In normal chainsaw use, replace the sprocket each time you replace the chain. You can rotate two new chains with one rim sprocket for longer sprocket life, but don't couple an old sprocket to a new chain or a new sprocket to an old chain—this will damage both sprocket and chain. You can see the damage in photos 3 (right) and 4.

Fuel—Lumbermaking puts heavy stress on a saw engine, so for extra lubrication I use a lower ratio of gas to oil than is recommended by the saw manufacturer. If the manufacturer calls for twenty-four parts gas to one part oil, for example, I use twenty parts gas to one part oil.

Use the oil and gas recommended by the manufacturer of your saw, especially during the saw's warranty period. When the recommended oil wasn't available, I've used snowmobile oil made for 2-cycle, air-cooled engines. Never use outboard engine 2-cycle quick mix, detergent, nondetergent or multigrade oils in your saw, because these cannot cope with the heat range of air-cooled chainsaw engines. Some chainsaw dealers stock new oils that suggest gas-to-oil ratios of fifty and even one hundred to one. Should you feel that these offer advantages, experiment with caution. I haven't tested them.

Clean fuel and good mixing procedures are a must. I've found that a five-gallon, plastic container with an internal, fine-screen spout and capped vent is the best. Metal containers tend to generate water from condensation and rust when not kept completely full.

Before fueling up, empty and clean the plastic container. Then pour in the proper amount of oil and add about a quarter of the amount of gasoline required. Shake well, add the rest of the gasoline and shake well again. Shake the container before every fill-up to mix the oil and gas.

1

2

3

4

Never smoke when refueling or checking the fuel tank. A partially filled tank is like a Molotov cocktail—the smallest spark can ignite it.

Occasionally, when a saw is mounted for milling, the fuel filter inside the gas tank will become dislodged in an upright position. This causes the engine to falter when you pull the throttle trigger and makes the engine sound as if it's not getting enough fuel. To check for this, wipe any sawdust or debris away from the fuel tank cap and remove it. Then drain the tank and inspect it to see if the filter is positioned properly. If the filter is dislodged, hold the saw upright and let the filter drop to the bottom of the tank before refueling.

Fouled fuel filters impede the proper flow of gas and should be removed. Take a short piece of wire and bend a crook in one end. (Some saw manufacturers supply such a tool with their tool kits.) Then insert the wire into the tank and gently pull out the filter unit (1). Remove the cap that covers the screened filter holder and take the filter out of its housing (2). Inspect it for water or dirt. You can wash a dirty filter in fuel mix, but I usually just replace it with a new one. Put back the filter cap and put the unit into the fuel tank. Make sure it drops to its proper position at the bottom. Gently screw on the fuel tank cap, making sure it is properly threaded. Do not overtighten it.

Fuel tank caps sometimes leak through the venting hole when the saw is mounted for milling. Usually, this is caused by a factory defect. Have your dealer replace the cap until you get one that works properly. It's not a good idea to plug a leaky venting hole because this creates a vacuum in the fuel tank, which puts a lot of stress on the fuel-pump diaphragms in the carburetor.

Chain oil—High-quality chain oil is essential for good lubrication. Chain oil is unlike ordinary oil in that it is specially made to penetrate to the rivet flanges and drive-link tails of the chain, while sticking to the bar rails, groove and nose.

Some manufacturers supply both a light-viscosity winter oil and a heavy-viscosity summer oil, while others supply just one. Heavy oil is sometimes thought to be less prone to fly off the chain, but I believe it also has less chance of penetrating to the rivets inside the drive links. This results in inadequate oiling, which can cause the chain to wear excessively, stiffen or break. I use a light-viscosity oil year round. Re-refined, light-viscosity oil gives excellent results, inexpensively. My favorite oil is SAE 10 hydraulic.

If I have to use a heavy-viscosity oil, I dilute it with diesel fuel so that the automatic chain oiler can function adequately. A chain oiler is functioning adequately if the drive links always show a film of oil, and the oil tank doesn't empty before the gas tank. If the automatic oiler on your saw has an adjustable flow control, open it as wide as possible for milling, without letting the oil tank go dry before the gas tank. If the oil tank has run dry and the oiler has an auxiliary manual pump, prime it by pumping before engine start-up. You should also pump the oiler before starting the mill into each cut because it provides a surplus of oil, and a well-oiled start prolongs chain and bar life.

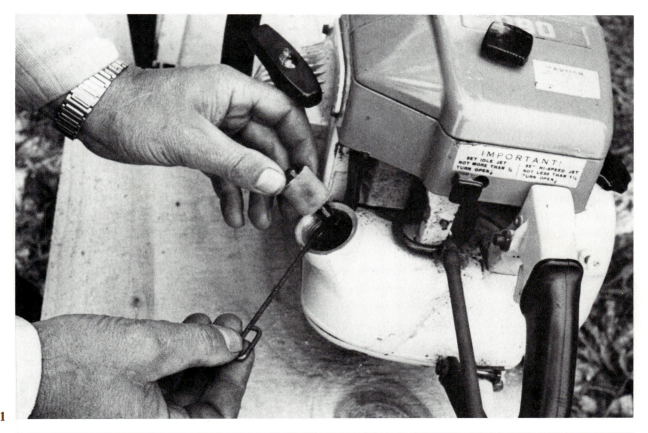

1

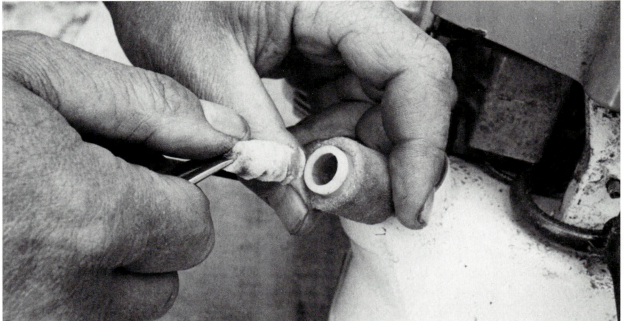

2

The Sawbar

The bar of a saw supports and guides the chain. As ripping places great stress on a sawbar, it is especially important that the bar used in lumbermaking be made of good-quality, hard steel. Soft steel wears quickly and can cause a number of problems. I think Cannon (Cannon Machine Works, 6337 Laurel, Burnaby, B.C., Canada V5B 3P3) makes the best bars, but a variety of manufacturers and designs exist (1).

To lighten the saw, chainsaw bars manufactured today are narrower in design. A narrow bar will work well with a mill up to 30 in. wide, but it will sag in the middle if the mill is improperly mounted to it. For mills over 30 in., I use a custom-built bar wide enough to support the additional length.

Bar noses—Bars are available with a choice of noses. In this photo (2), the first bar on the left has an internally mounted bearing-sprocket nose. The second bar has a nose with an insert of steel harder than the bar welded to its edge. The third bar has a new style bearing-sprocket nose and the fourth bar has a bearing-roller nose.

I use a bar with a bearing-roller or bearing-sprocket nose because the bearing reduces the amount of friction between bar and chain and allows the chain to cut with up to 20 percent more power. A sprocket or roller supports the chain away from the bar and helps eliminate bar-end wear. The pitch on bearing-sprocket and bearing-roller noses must match the pitch of the chain and engine sprocket. The fraction marked on the bar that is third from the left in the photo shows the pitch of the nose.

When a mill is mounted to a bar, it must be positioned so as not to impede the work of the bar nose. The bar should be 4 in. to 6 in. longer than the length of the mill.

Bar ends—Bar-end designs vary (3), but all have elements in common. Slots allow movement of the bar for chain tensioning, the large holes accommodate the chain-tension pin, and the small holes allow oil passage from the engine to the chain. Make sure the bar you select has the proper mounting configuration for your saw.

1

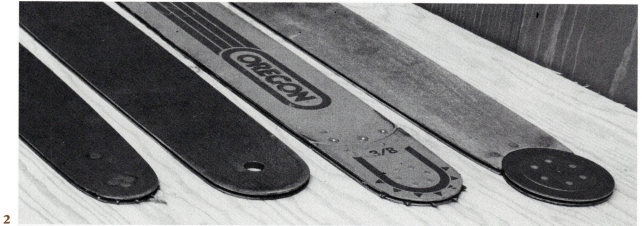

2

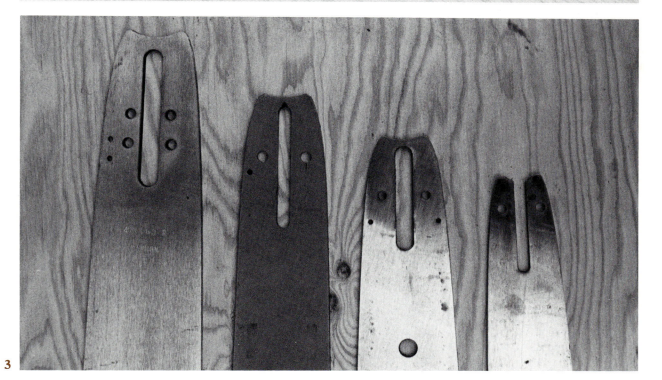

3

Bar maintenance—The bottom edge of a bar usually leads into the cut, and so receives the most wear. To balance wear, flip the bar top to bottom after about 20 hours of operation. Always make sure before remounting that the oil hole is clean.

In proper operation, the tie straps of the chain slide along the bar rails. But as the bar rails in this photo wore down (**1**), the drive links of the chain started to ride on the bottom of the bar groove, plowing it out. This ruined the chain and burned the bar. The point is: With regular bar inspection and maintenance, this problem could have been avoided.

As the chain slides along the bar rails and the bar begins to wear, a burr can form along the rail edge (**2**), causing improper chain tracking. Square the rails by draw-filing (**3**). Support the file on two blocks of wood, each positioned square to the top of the bar. Hold the file as shown in the photo.

If the rails have become too hard for draw-filing, a metal-cutting wheel mounted in a Skilsaw or table saw will do the job (**4**). Mount the wheel 90° to the saw table and lightly pass the bar against the wheel in gentle, steady strokes the full length of the bar on both sides. A properly squared bar will balance on its edge on a level surface.

I use a belt sander to clean the sides of the bar and to remove any burrs there (**5**). Sand evenly over the entire surface. If you don't have a belt sander, use a flat file.

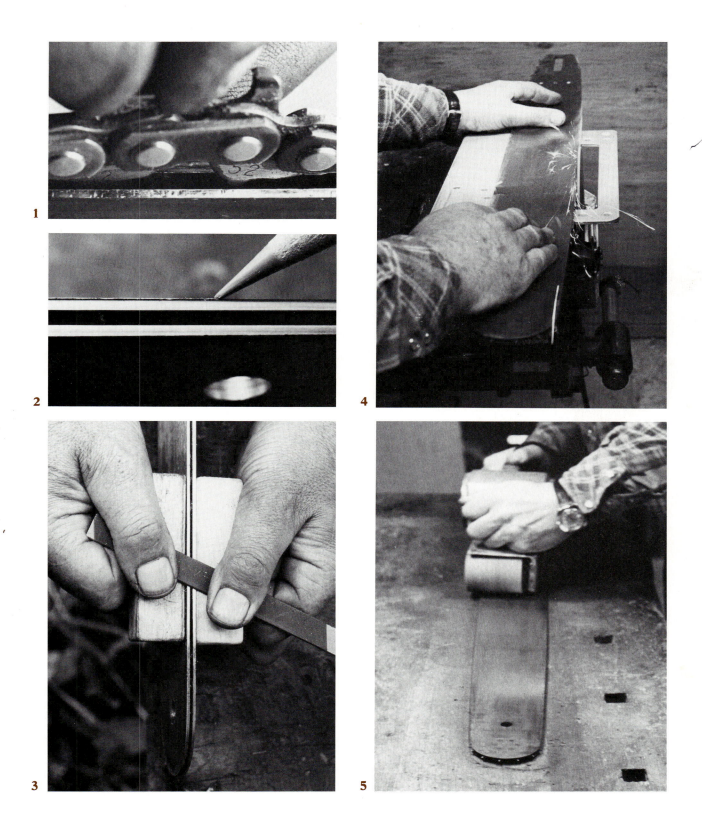

1

2

3

4

5

Also on the bar-maintenance checklist should be a periodic check of bar-groove width, also called bar gauge. With feeler gauges, measure groove width all around the bar (1), and compare this measurement with the known gauge of the bar.

To determine the amount of wear, subtract the new width from the original width. For example, if the new measurement is .072 in. and the original gauge was .063, the wear is .009 in. Worn bars can be rehammered and regrooved by bar-repair shops. I usually send mine in when wear exceeds .010 in.

Bar-groove depth also needs to be checked regularly. If you have a bar-groove measuring tool (2,3), use it to check at intervals around the bar. If you don't have one, use a matchstick or anything else that will fit easily in the groove. Compare the length of the bottom of a drive link (4) to groove depth; there should be space between the bottom of the drive links and the bottom of the bar groove. This distance reveals remaining bar life.

Engine Modification

An engine sawdust guard (5) does several jobs. It holds the guide plate that controls chain entry into the bar and it is also the clamping bracket for the bar. In normal crosscutting, the guard allows sawdust to be directed away from the saw through a bottom opening.

However, when the saw is inverted in the milling position, the opening doesn't allow the sawdust to escape properly, which causes a sawdust buildup between the centrifugal clutch and the guard. This often leads to internal clutch problems and heavy clutch-shoe wear.

An easy modification eliminates this problem. Simply cut away the sawdust-shielding portion of the unit (6) and use the guide plate and clamping bracket as you normally would. This exposes additional moving parts, but because the saw is inverted during milling, the advantages make it worthwhile to me.

With this modification, you also won't have to remove the bar from the engine to mount or remove the chain.

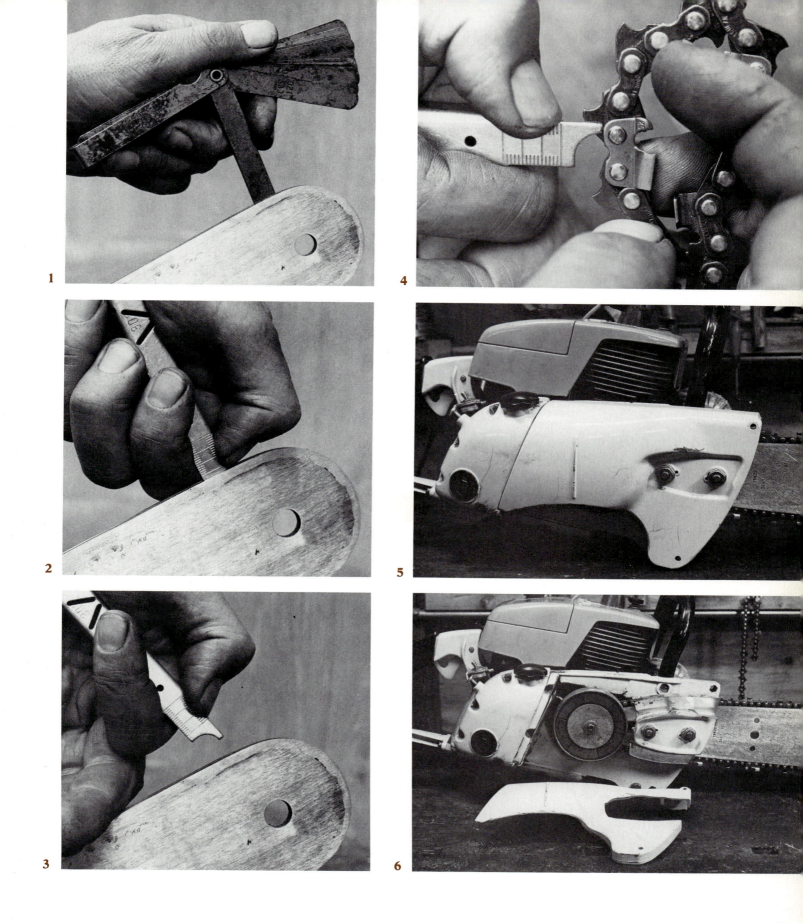

1

2

3

4

5

6

Chapter 3

Ripping Chain

The most important factor in successful lumbermaking is properly prepared and maintained chain. Although you can use standard crosscutting chain, this will result in inefficient milling. You really need ripping chain, and in the early 1960s I invented and patented ripping chain especially for chainsaw lumbermaking. This chain is made by modifying crosscut chain and is sold today by various manufacturers of portable mills.

Over the years I grew dissatisfied with the inefficiency of the original, patented ripping chain, so I continued my research. Today I have what I consider to be the ultimate chain for lumbermaking (1). This new chain is not yet available commercially, but you can modify your own chain at home, using either a grinder or a hand file. I usually use Oregon square-edge chisel chain (model 52L) made by Omark (Oregon Saw Chain Division, 9701 S.E. McLoughlin Blvd., Portland, Ore. 97222) for .063-in. gauge bars with .404-in. pitch. I've never had any success modifying round or chamfered-edge chain. I also don't recommend using safety chain. Safety chain is designed to prevent the nose of the bar from kicking back when crosscutting, but when ripping, the guard links prevent good sawdust clearance and adequate sawdust flow.

It's not hard to modify chain, but first you must have a working knowledge of its components. Chains have several variable features: pitch, gauge and number of tie straps between each cutter.

Chain pitch is the distance between the centers of one rivet and the rivet after the next, divided by two. The saw sprocket and the bar-nose sprocket (if your bar has one) must have the same pitch as the chain.

Chain gauge is measured by the thickness of the bottom of the drive links, which ride in the groove of the bar. Chain gauge must be coordinated with bar gauge.

Regular chain has a single tie strap separating each cutter; skip-tooth chain has two tie straps. I always use regular chain because a single tie strap gives better support to the cutters. While skip-tooth chain has fewer cutters to be modified and sharpened, I find it does not cut as smoothly or as efficiently.

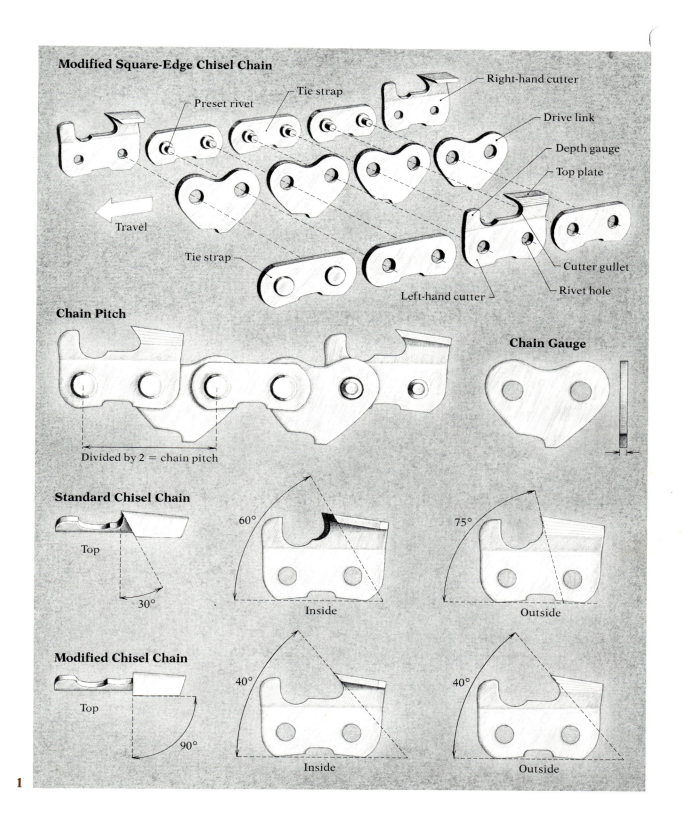

Modified Square-Edge Chisel Chain

Right-hand cutter
Preset rivet
Tie strap
Drive link
Depth gauge
Top plate
Travel
Tie strap
Cutter gullet
Left-hand cutter
Rivet hole

Chain Pitch

Divided by 2 = chain pitch

Chain Gauge

Standard Chisel Chain

Top
30°
60°
Inside
75°
Outside

Modified Chisel Chain

Top
90°
40°
Inside
40°
Outside

1

Chain Assembly

I prefer to purchase chain in bulk (rolls of 25, 50 or 100 ft.), because it's usually less expensive than preassembled chain. When working with bulk chain, you need to know the length needed for the saw and bar you're using. Chain length is often referred to by the number of drive links rather than by measured length. When the model number of a chain manufactured for a particular saw is followed by a dash and another number—for example, 52L-70E—the last number (70E) refers to chain length (which means the chain has 70 drive links). Most saw dealers have length charts that give the number of links necessary for the saw and bar you're using.

Of course, you can also determine chain length by counting the drive links of an existing chain for your saw. Or you can retract the sawbar and thread the chain around the bar. Mark the tie strap where the chain ends meet, which is where the chain must be broken. Then rivet the ends of the chain together to form a continuous loop.

There are various ways to dismantle and reconstruct chain. Several types of chain breakers and spin riveters are available, and although some of these work well if you follow the directions, others don't. I prefer to use my own system.

To begin, clamp the tie strap square in the jaws of a vise at the point where the chain is to be broken. File the two rivet heads flush with the tie strap side (1), or grind the heads flush on a grindstone (I usually do this freehand). Remount the chain in the vise, clamping the drive links, and complete the break by applying a little sideways pressure to the strap (2). You could also use a punch to complete the break. (Wear gloves when handling chain, especially if you are unaccustomed to working with it.) Discard the dismantled tie strap (3) and use a new one to assemble the chain. Always break chain on a tie strap, but if you have to break at a cutter, assemble the chain using a new tie strap instead of a new cutter.

1

2

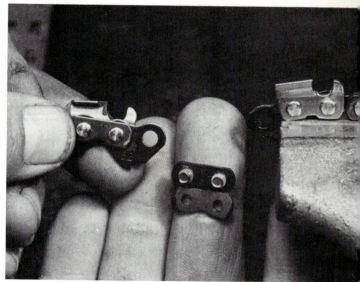

3

Occasionally it's necessary to break a used chain to repair or shorten it. Chain tends to stretch with use, and you'll have to shorten it when it stretches beyond your saw's tensioning capacity. But because tie strap width decreases with wear, you'll have to adjust the new tie strap to match the used ones before assembling the chain. First, measure the width of one used tie strap (**1**), then file the bottoms of the new straps to the width of the used one (**2**). Failure to do this can result in excessive bar wear and erratic cutting.

To assemble chain, place a preset tie strap (the one with the rivets attached) on the bottom (**3**). Direct the rivets up through the drive links being connected. Place a regular tie strap over the rivets. I use vise-grips to hold the two tie straps together for peening on an anvil (**4**). Peen the rivets gently, using the ball part of a machinist's ball-peen hammer. Then reset the vise-grips onto one of the connecting drive links for access to both rivets, and continue peening until the head is formed (**5**).

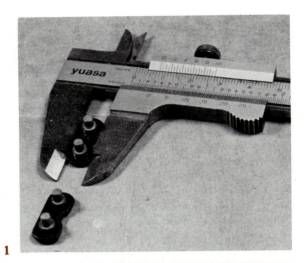

1

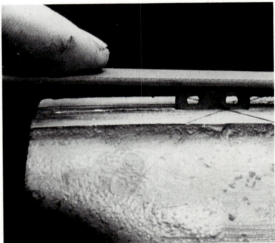

2

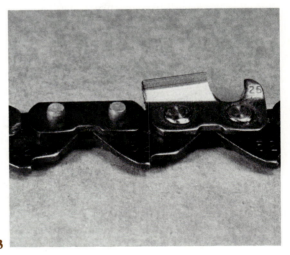

3

4

5

The Grinder

You'll find that a good disc-wheel chain grinder (1) will soon pay for itself by its accuracy in modifying and sharpening ripping chain. Although you can use hand files to modify chain (p. 32), one grinding stone will do the work of several dozen files. The grinder is also the only tool able to sharpen cutters whose edges have become crystallized by contact with sand, rocks and metal. I like to use the Jolly Chain Grinder, made by Windsor Machine Co. Ltd. (3147 Thunderbird Crescent, Burnaby, B.C., Canada (V5A 3G1).

Most grinders come equipped with two stones—a fine-grit stone for grinding and sharpening chain cutters and a coarse-grit stone for grinding depth gauges. I prefer to use a coarse-grit stone for initial chain modification and a fine-grit stone for sharpening. But regardless of the grit, all grindstones tend to clog, which can cause the chain cutters to burn. I have experimented with various stone lubricants, and have found that paraffin is the best one. Rubbing a block of paraffin or a paraffin candle on the spinning stone frequently (at least several times per chain) not only reduces clogging substantially, but also reduces the number of times you need to dress the stone (2).

Stone thickness is not critical when sharpening ripping chain because the most important part of the grind is done with the side of the stone. But in initial chain modification, it's best to use a stone that is thick enough to remove the total amount of metal necessary in one pass. Stone shape, however, is important. To produce the correct cutter shape (p. 26), you'll have to establish a flat edge on the stone for grinding the bottoms of the cutter gullets and a rounded edge for shaping the round part of the gullet.

Although I'm using a carborundum stone dresser in these photos, I prefer to use a star-wheel dresser to shape the stone. Star-wheel dressers actually cut away the stone, while carborundum dressers (and the diamond dressers built into some grinders) tend to clog it up. For a good cut that produces a crisp edge, you need a sharp, clean, grinding surface.

Shape the flat edge of the stone by setting the grinder cutting arm at 50° from vertical. Use the chain track on the grinder to control the movement of the carborundum stone dresser or star wheel (3). Pull the grinder arm down gently to bring the stone into contact with the dresser, and slide the dresser from side to side on the chain track—in this way, the bottom of the stone is ground parallel to the chain track.

To form the rounded edge, hold the dresser freehand against the leading edge of the stone (4). With short, controlled sweeps, round the edge. Wear safety glasses when using a grinder to protect your eyes from flying debris.

1

2

3

4

Chain Modification

Regular chain, beveled across the fronts of the cutters at 30°, enters the kerf at an angle, which can cause excessive side pressure on cutters and drive links. When chain is ground this way, the corner of each cutter becomes the prime cutting area; once that area dulls, cutting ability is greatly reduced. To solve this problem, I grind my ripping chain cutters straight across the fronts with the shaped grinding stone adjusted 50° from vertical (40° from horizontal). This is the way commercial sawmills grind their blades for circular saws, gangsaws and bandsaws.

To modify chain, first adjust the grinder so the stone is 90° to the chain, then tilt the stone to a 50° hook angle. Mount a square-edge chisel crosscut chain in the chain track and advance the chain so that the back of a cutter touches the tip of the pawl (1). You can start with either a right-hand or a left-hand cutter, as this system allows left and right cutters to be ground one after another.

Bring down the stone and adjust the pawl backward or forward so the top of the stone will grind off the entire angled edge of the cutter—no more and no less. Then lock the cutter into position, pushing it up against the pawl. Start the grinder, and with a firm grip on the grinder arm, lower the stone gently so that it starts to cut (2). Check to be sure you are only grinding off the complete preground angle. If you have to, slack off on the lock handle and readjust the pawl.

Grind with short strokes until the bottom of the stone comes to just above the tops of the drive links (3). Then let up on the grinder arm so the stone can rise. Shut off the motor, and when the stone has stopped spinning, lower the arm until the stone comes down to the bottom of the new grind. Lock the stone in that position so all the cutters will be ground to the same depth.

Now release the pressure on the grinder arm and allow the stone to return to its out-of-cut position. Examine the cutter tooth—notice how the edge of the stone has made a straight cut down the front of the cutter (4). The rounded part of the stone has formed a gullet that is not only stronger than a sharp-angled gullet, but also will help direct the flow of sawdust. Also notice the amount of metal removed. The gauge in this photo (5) reads 40° from horizontal, which is 50° from vertical.

Repeat the process, pushing the next cutter up against the pawl. After grinding, examine the cutter to be sure it has the same grind as the previous one. Check frequently as you progress to make sure all adjustments are properly set.

As the grinding stone becomes glazed, retouch it with the stone dresser. With continued use, the flat side of the stone will wear, causing the grinding angle to drop below 50°. A decrease of a degree or two isn't important, but if the angle drops to 45°, you can compensate with an increase in the angle of the arm of the grinder. Or, dress off the flat edge of the stone and round off the leading edge, as in basic stone modification (p. 24).

1

2

4

3

5

Sharpening

A dull chain is usually the cause of power loss and poor cutting in milling. Sharpen the chain as soon as it shows the slightest sign of dulling. The top edge of a cutter will not reflect light if it is sharp, but a dull edge will shine.

Use either the chain grinder or a file to maintain the shape and edge on your chain. Cutters dulled in normal use require only a little grinding to restore sharpness. You can use the same coarse-grit grinding stone for sharpening as you did for cutter modification, or a fine-grit stone (lubricated with paraffin to retard clogging), modified to the correct shape.

Mount the chain in the grinder, then adjust the pawl so the stone can pass into the cutter gullet with zero clearance between the stone and the top edge of the cutter (1). The chain should be positioned so that the stone just brushes past the edge of the cutter. Gently lower the stone into the gullet and adjust its depth stop.

To make a sharpening pass, start the grinder and lower the stone to the bottom of the gullet, applying slight sideways pressure on the grinding arm toward the cutter (2). At the bottom of the gullet, release the sideways pressure to allow the stone to rise out of the cut. If you don't do this, you'll get a large burr on the cutting edge. You'll also get a large burr if the stone has become glazed.

Now examine the cutter to be sure it has been completely sharpened. The shiny, dull edge should be completely gone, leaving a sharp edge that will not reflect light.

If cutters are severely damaged, you'll have to adjust the grinder to remove the whole damaged area on the top plate of each cutter (3). Use the most damaged cutter in the chain as a gauge to adjust the pawl. This will ensure that the damage on all the cutters will be removed, and that they will be ground to the same length and sharpness. When excessive grinding is necessary, always check the depth-gauge height (p. 30).

For sharpening chain on the bar, I like to use a Simington sharpener (Simington Products Co., Star Route 141, Chiloquin, Ore. 97624). It's battery-powered and can go right into the woods with you (4). A 12-volt motorcycle battery will power many sharpenings on a single charge. Though there are a variety of motor-powered, on-the-bar chain grinders available, I don't recommend them—they are inefficient and, above all, inaccurate.

1

2

3

4

Depth Gauges

The depth gauge controls the cutting depth of each cutter (**1**). All depth gauges should be set at the same height so that an equal workload can be carried by all the cutters. When measuring new chain, I've often found depth gauges that are more than .010 in. off, which causes cutting inefficiency as well as chain, bar and sprocket wear.

The proper height for depth gauges varies with the species of tree to be cut, log size, engine power and bar length. For ripping, I usually set depth gauges about five or ten thousandths of an inch more than is recommended for the crosscutting chain I've modified. For example, with a Stihl 090 and a 52L Oregon chain, I normally use a .045-in. depth-gauge clearance. Set the depth gauges only after the chain has been modified; check and file them down, if necessary, after about every fourth or fifth chain sharpening.

To check depth-gauge setting, use a depth-gauge tool. These come in a number of styles and at a variety of preset depths. I prefer a depth-gauge tool with the filing slot in the center, which allows you to use both hands on the file. A tool with the filing slot on an end must be held with one hand as you file with the other. With the chain on the bar, mount the tool with its slot positioned over a depth gauge (**2**). If the depth gauge protrudes above the slot, it needs to be filed down. Use a 6-in. mill bastard file until it won't cut anymore (**3**). The area around the slot is harder than the file can cut, so you won't hurt the tool or over-cut the depth gauge.

After filing, move the chain forward so that the next depth gauge is in the same position on the bar. It is important to file each depth gauge in the same location because curvature in the bar can cause variations in depth-gauge readings. Complete the filing of all the depth gauges on the chain, then, with the same file, round off the lead corner of each depth gauge to original factory shape (**4,5**). I usually do this freehand.

Depth-Gauge Setting

To determine depth-gauge setting, measure the distance between a straightedge set on top of two cutters on the same side of the chain and the top of the depth gauge. All gauges should be set to the same height.

Straightedge — Cutting depth —

1

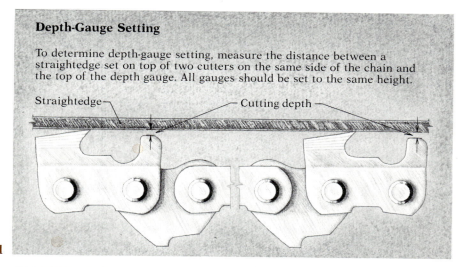

2

3

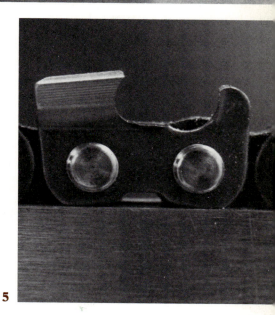

4

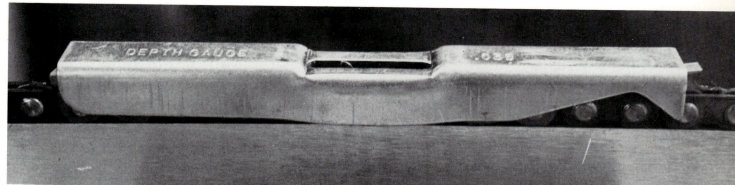

5

Hand-Filing

Chain modification with a file guide and round file is essentially the same as with a grinder, but when modifying by hand, I file a 45° hook on each cutter instead of a 50° hook. This is because the round file leaves an edge that is hollow-ground; if the hook were filed to 50°, the cutting edge would be weakened.

To modify my .404-pitch, .063-gauge 52L Oregon chain, I use the Oregon model #25892 file guide and a $\frac{7}{32}$-in. round file. Start off with the file diameter recommended for your chain, but switch to the next smallest size ($\frac{1}{32}$ in. less) when the cutters of the chain are about half-worn. Don't assume the file guide will be straight when you take it out of the package—check yours and straighten it out if necessary.

The file guide, as it comes from the manufacturer, is set to file a hook angle of approximately 5°—to increase the angle, it is necessary to shim the file in the guide at both ends, directly under both clamps (1). I usually use two or three strips of a matchbook cover to start, adding strips until the file cuts a 45° hook. It's a good idea to start with a conservative number of strips, to avoid removing too much metal. For an example of shim thickness, with the $\frac{7}{32}$-in. file and guide I'm using here, the shim measures .060 in.

When hand-filing in the shop (and especially for initial chain modification), I prefer to hold the chain in a small machinist's vise, rather than to file while the chain is on the bar. (When sharpening in the field, when the chain is on the bar, I mount the bar in a holder made especially for field work.) With a square, draw a line 90° across the jaws of the vise, then mount your chain. Position the file guide flat on top of the first cutter, touching the depth gauge, and keep the guide parallel to the line (2).

With both hands, file in long, controlled strokes, using the full length of the file. Don't drag the file on the back stroke, as this will wear it out. Remember to keep the guide flat on top of the cutter. Keep filing until the hook angle on the side of the cutter is 45° and the top plate is 90° across (3). The bottom of the cutter gullet should be just above the tops of the drive links. To speed things up, I sometimes file the cutter back freehand, then use the guide to complete the modification accurately.

As you modify your chain, measure the length of the top plate of the cutters to make sure that they are all exactly the same. You can use a crescent wrench or caliper for a gauge.

It's a good idea to rotate the file in the guide slightly as you feel it start to dull. At least two files will usually be necessary to modify one chain. Never use a dull file to modify or sharpen chain—it's a waste of time.

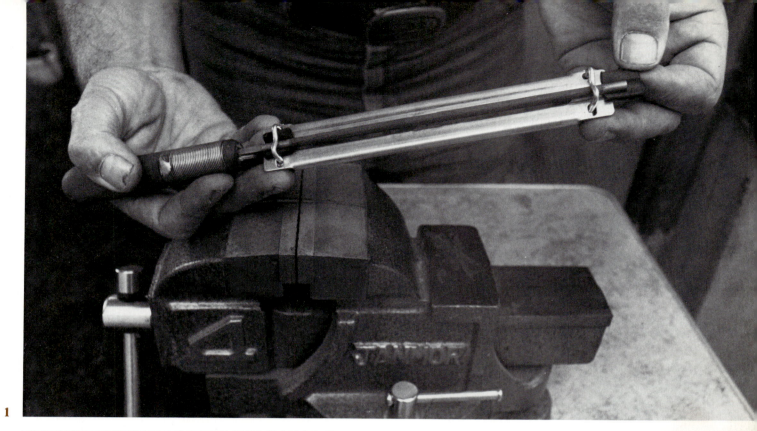

1

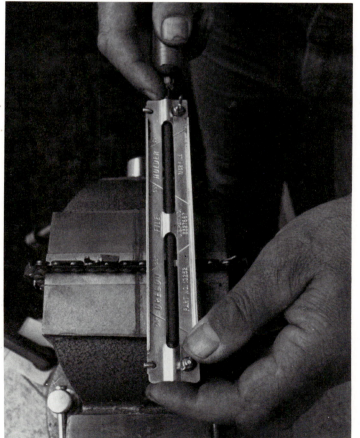

2

3

33

Chapter 4

Mill Selection and Assembly

When selecting a chainsaw lumbermaking device, consider the size of the logs you plan to mill, as well as your type of chainsaw and the bar length. For many of my milling needs, I use a Granberg Mark III Alaskan Mill (Granberg Industries Ltd., 202 S. Garrard Blvd., Richmond, Calif. 94804) **(1)**. These come in a variety of sizes from 24 in. to 56 in.; I find the most efficient mills are 48 in. and under.

The Mark III mill is lightweight, reasonably durable, accurate and inexpensive. It also has flat-bottomed, sliding guide rails, which scrape the sawdust from the milled surface as they go. (The fine sawdust not scraped away acts as a lubricant.) Roller guide rails, common on many types of mills, roll up over wood chips and sawdust, resulting in an irregular cut. If you're using a mill with roller guide rails, make a point of keeping the milling surface free of debris as you go.

If you purchase a mill, and it's not assembled, inspect the components against the parts list and drawings supplied by the manufacturer before you do anything else. Then lay out the components in the approximate order of assembly, checking each for twist, bend or warp. Correct any defects you find, and if a component is beyond repair, have it replaced.

Lubricate often-used nut and bolt threads with a good lubricant, such as Never-Seez or a mixture of grease and graphite, to allow for proper torquing and adjustment. The lubricant helps reduce thread wear and also retards rust and corrosion. Then assemble the mill, following instructions carefully. Take your time—haste can lead to damaged or misaligned parts.

When the mill is assembled, double-check to be sure you've followed all procedures properly before taking the mill into the field. Remember, precision in the shop is vital to productive and enjoyable work in the field.

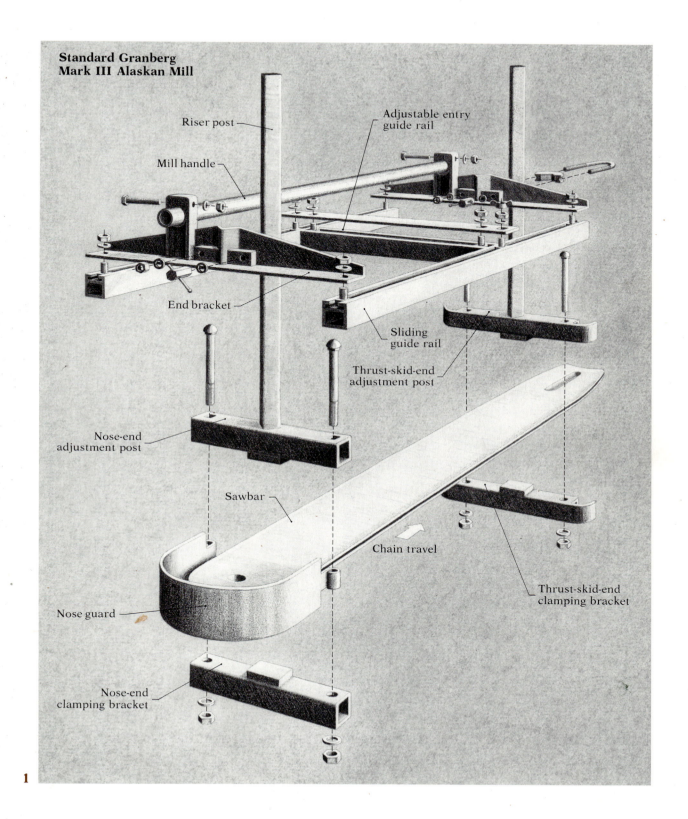

**Standard Granberg
Mark III Alaskan Mill**

Riser post

Adjustable entry
guide rail

Mill handle

End bracket

Sliding
guide rail

Thrust-skid-end
adjustment post

Nose-end
adjustment post

Sawbar

Chain travel

Thrust-skid-end
clamping bracket

Nose guard

Nose-end
clamping bracket

1

Mounting the mill—To mount the mill on the sawbar, slack off the bar nuts and loosen the chain. Retract the bar as far as possible and draw a line across the bar where it meets the saw. This line marks the farthest point at which the mill can be mounted on the engine end of the bar. (If you're using the engine for both crosscutting and ripping, and are leaving the felling spikes on the saw, mark at the end of the spikes.)

Return the bar to its working position, readjust chain tension and secure the bar clamping nuts. Mark the tip of the bar at a point that will allow space between the bar and the nose guard or helper handle. The two vertical lines in the photograph **(1)** mark the maximum limits for mounting the mill on this bar.

Before mounting, set the height of the mill to 3 in. on both riser posts. Then mount the mill within the marked lines, as close to the engine as possible. If the mill is mounted too far forward, the weight of the engine could cause the bar to flex or the chain to track improperly, resulting in a bowed cut or even a bent bar.

After mounting, check that the bar is straight by laying a straightedge against it lengthwise or by sighting down the bar—a twisted or sagging bar can be a power robber. Then raise the mill setting to maximum cutting height, making sure to move both end brackets evenly up the riser posts. Double-check that the bar is straight by sighting down it **(2)** or using the straightedge. If the bar isn't straight at the maximum setting, loosen a mill-handle bolt at one end of the mill and the two guide-rail bolts at the same end. Adjust the mill handle until the saw straightens.

With all components in proper position, the mill aligned, and all nuts and bolts torqued, the standard mill is ready to go. But first let's have a look at a few other things you might want to do.

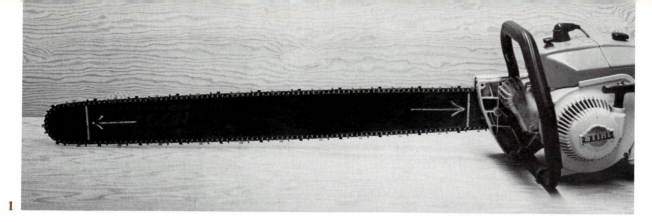

1

2

Mill Modification

Thrust skid—The thrust skid of the Mark III Alaskan Mill has a built-in design problem. It often loses contact with the log **(1)**, which causes the riser post to touch the side of the log, and quite often, to get hung up. The heavy vibration and stress exerted on the riser posts, guide rails and mill handle can also result in parts breaking or bending, or in misalignment of the mill.

Here's one simple solution to the problem. Mount another thrust-skid unit inboard. Purchase these Mark III parts **(2)**: #790 clamping bracket (thrust-skid end); #788 clamping bracket (nose end); two #808 $5/16''$ x $3\frac{1}{2}''$ carriage bolts; two #684 $5/16$-in. hex nuts. Epoxy small strips of cloth-backed sandpaper (from a worn, coarse sanding belt) to the steel pads on the brackets to prevent the thrust skid from slipping on the bar. Bolt the unit on where needed **(3)**.

There's another problem with the standard thrust skid—it often gets caught on a log's surface irregularities, causing the mill to jog and cut unevenly. I therefore find it necessary to use an additional thrust skid **(4)** that is much longer than the standard skid. You can make it from 1-in.-square steel tube if available, but angle iron will also do quite well. Heat the end of the tube and bend it while holding it in a vise. Hacksaw a slightly curved line for the nose and another line for the shoe. Remove the wedge of metal between the lines and pound the shoe up around the nose. Trim off the excess and weld or braze the nose and shoe together. Drill two $3/8$-in. holes in the new skid to align with the holes in the standard skid, and attach it to the mill.

The extra length and curved end of this thrust skid ensure smooth mill travel over log irregularities. The photograph **(5)** shows the thrust skid in action.

1

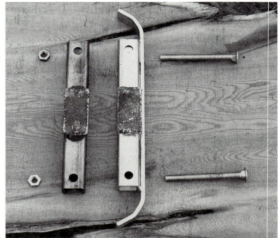

2

3

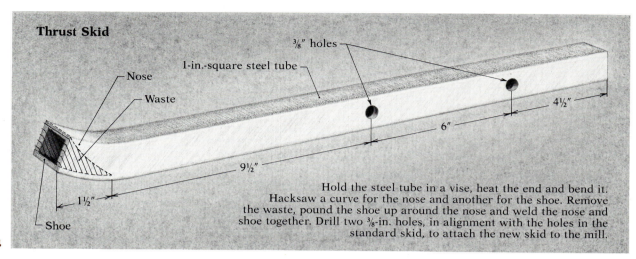

Thrust Skid

Nose

Waste

Shoe

1½"

9½"

1-in.-square steel tube

⅜" holes

6"

4½"

Hold the steel tube in a vise, heat the end and bend it. Hacksaw a curve for the nose and another for the shoe. Remove the waste, pound the shoe up around the nose and weld the nose and shoe together. Drill two ⅜-in. holes, in alignment with the holes in the standard skid, to attach the new skid to the mill.

4

5

Bolting on the mill—The standard Mark III Alaskan Mill clamps onto the chainsaw bar. This design lets you use the same bar for both crosscutting and milling by simply clamping on the mill, but to replace a dull chain with a sharp one, you have to remove the entire mill unit. So I use a separate bar or another saw for crosscutting and modify my mill so that it bolts onto the milling bar. This lets me change chains while the mill remains mounted.

Here's how to modify a mill for bolting on. Drill and tap ½-in. holes dead center on both riser posts (1). On the thrust-skid (engine) end of the mill, drill and tap two ⁵⁄₁₆-holes, each at a distance of ¾ in. from the center of the first hole. On both ends of the mill, drill out the two existing ⁵⁄₁₆-in. holes in the adjustment posts and clamping brackets to ⅜ in., to accommodate ⅜″ x 4″ bolts. These bolts are long enough to accept spacer nuts between the modified thrust skid and the sawbar, while leaving enough space to remove the chain. The bolts also hold the sawbar nose guard in place on the mill (2).

To modify the sawbar to accept the mill, measure the distance between the centers of the ½-in. holes in the riser posts with mill height set to 3 in. Mark and center-punch the bar for two corresponding holes.

On the engine end of the bar, mark and center-punch two ⁵⁄₁₆-in. holes, each at a distance of ¾ in. from the center of the ½-in. hole.

Drill the bar holes at very low speed with a good-quality, high-speed drill or a carbide-tipped masonry drill. Be sure to have an old bar or a piece of flatstock iron under the bar, to drill into (3). This is the secret to drilling bars. If you drill into the hole in the drill-press bed or into a wooden support block (as is normal metalworking procedure), the drill would just start through the bar and the unfinished hole would harden because of the air-hardening qualities of bar steel. You'd end up with an unfinished, hardened hole and a burnt-out or broken drill bit. (Should this ever happen to you, grind out the hardened hole with a round stone in a high-speed grinder.)

1

2

3

41

The Mill

Assembling the mill—When mounting the sawbar, be sure the mounting areas of saw, bar and guard are clean. Oiler holes on saw and bar (1) should be free of obstructions. Fit the bar on the studs and over the chain-tension pin, and clamp the bar to the engine with the clamping bracket. Tighten the nuts.

Bolt the bar to the riser posts through the ½-in. holes with ⁷⁄₁₆″ x 1¼″ bolts (2). Use an extra heavy, ½-in. flat washer under the bolthead for a good torquing base. On the thrust-skid end of the mill, insert ⁵⁄₁₆″ x ¾″ bolts and washers through the bar and into the holes. These bolts add support and compensate for the extra pressure the long thrust skid will put on the post. It's a good idea to use thread lubricant on all nuts and bolts.

Now pass two ⅜″ x 4″ bolts through the holes in the adjustment post on the thrust-skid end of the mill. Screw four ⅜-in. nuts on each bolt and torque them down. Put the long thrust skid over the bolts and lock it with two more nuts. Torque the skid down with the first nut and use the second to lock the first.

On the nose end, pass two ⅜″ x 4″ bolts through the adjustment post and nose guard. Screw on two ⅜-in. nuts on each bolt and install the clamping bracket with the pad inverted. On the non-cutting side of the bar, screw and torque two ⅜-in. spacer nuts. Then screw and torque one ⅜-in. nut on the bolt on the cutting side of the bar. Install a ⅜-in. flat washer and then a ⅜-in. lock washer, and torque down a ⅜-in. nut. This forms one of the winch buttons necessary to hold the ropes used in the winching setup. The other button is described on p. 50.

Once you've mounted the mill, make one final modification. Drill a ⅜-in. hole through the standard thrust skid in alignment with the chain-tension screw. With this modification, you can reach the screw easily with your screwdriver (3) and tension the chain while in the cut.

A properly mounted, modified mill and bar will not need to be removed for chain sharpening or maintenance, but you should flip the bar every 20 hours of operation to balance bar wear. Simply unbolt the bar from the modified mill and remount it upside down.

1

3

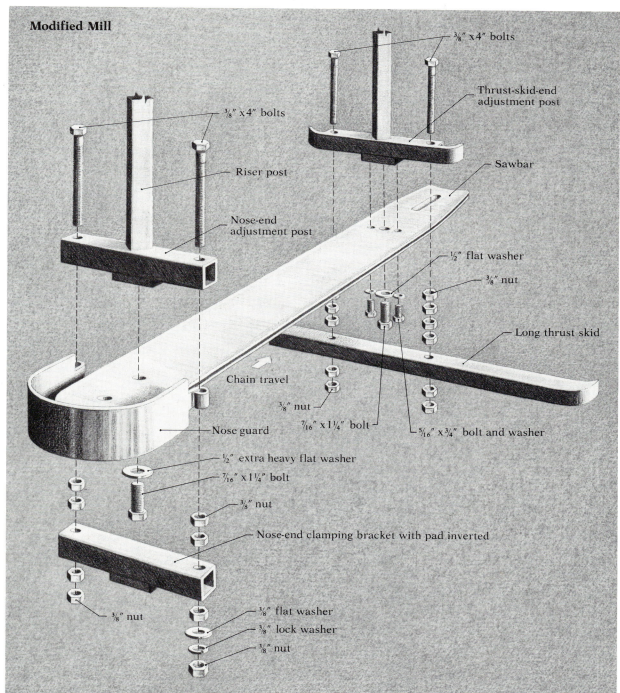

Modified Mill

⅜″ x 4″ bolts

⅜″ x 4″ bolts

Thrust-skid-end adjustment post

Riser post

Sawbar

Nose-end adjustment post

½″ flat washer

⅜″ nut

Long thrust skid

Chain travel

⅜″ nut

Nose guard

⁷⁄₁₆″ x 1¼″ bolt

⁵⁄₁₆″ x ¾″ bolt and washer

½″ extra heavy flat washer

⁷⁄₁₆″ x 1¼″ bolt

⅜″ nut

Nose-end clamping bracket with pad inverted

⅜″ nut

⅜″ flat washer

⅜″ lock washer

⅜″ nut

2

Mill-Mounting the Chain

After modification, it becomes quite simple to mount or remove chain from the saw.

To mount the chain **(1)**, retract the bar by slacking off about a half turn on the bar nuts, just enough to enable you to loosen the chain-tension screw. (Count the number of turns it takes to loosen the chain-tension screw and you'll find it easier to tension the chain later.) Hold the chain in the proper direction of travel and insert it behind the clutch and onto the chain sprocket. The chain should be going away from the saw engine at the top of the bar and toward the engine at the bottom.

Thread the chain through the space between the thrust skid and the bar **(2)**. Place the chain between the chain-guide plates and feed it through the thrust-skid space **(3)**.

Continue threading the chain, starting it in the groove around the nose **(4)**. Make sure the chain is properly positioned on top of the bar and all the way back to the engine, then advance the chain with your fingers so it drops into the groove. Tighten the chain on the bar as you feed it into the groove.

Now, holding the chain at the center of the bar top and bottom, move it a few revolutions around the bar to remove kinks. Then hold the chain at the center of the top of the bar and lift it up out of the groove. If the drive links just clear the top of the groove under normal finger pressure, and you can easily rotate the chain by hand, the chain is properly tensioned **(5)**.

With the tension set correctly, tighten the bar nuts **(6)**. Rotate the chain around the bar, lubricating it with the manual oiler as you go. Start the engine and run the chain a bit, then stop it and check the tension, adjusting if necessary. New chain tends to stretch on break-in, so check the tension again soon after you start milling.

Adjusting chain tension is an important maintenance procedure. Chain that is too loose can whip out of the bar groove; chain that is too tight can cause a rough cut and, if not checked, will wear out quickly.

The procedure for removing a chain is essentially the same as for putting it on. Slack the bar nuts about a half turn, just enough to loosen the chain by unscrewing the chain-tension screw. Lift the chain up out of the groove on top of the bar and pull it back a bit **(7)**. Rotate the chain around the bar a little and off the nose. When the chain is off the nose, thread it back along the bar. Slip it off the sprocket and out around the clutch.

Always be careful when handling chain.

1

4

2

5

3

6

7

Chapter 5

The Winch

In lumbermaking, you normally have to push the mill and roaring chainsaw through a cut, breathing exhaust fumes and spitting out sawdust all the while. But with my setup **(1)**, you can stand back from the noise and vibration, and move the saw through the cut with minimum labor—all you have to do is crank a winch handle. Besides the winch, you'll need a remote throttle attachment for your saw, winch buttons to hold the winching ropes and a winch yoke. I'll discuss each of these in turn.

You can make a winch from parts that are readily available. I use a small boat-trailer winch as the base mechanism. You'll also need an electric hand drill, a hacksaw and a bench grinder.

Make winch dogs (to attach the winch unit to the log) by tapering ⅜-in. bolts. Hold each bolt in the chuck of the drill and, with the drill switched on, grind the taper with a bench grinder **(2)**.

Assemble the winch **(3,4)** and mount the winch rope. Cut a length of ¼-in. or 5/16-in. nylon or polypropylene rope a little longer than double the length of the log you'll be milling, then splice or tie an eye to each end. Fold the rope in half and attach the fold to the winch drum. Later you'll thread the rope ends through the cheek blocks on the winch yoke (p. 92).

1

2

The Winch

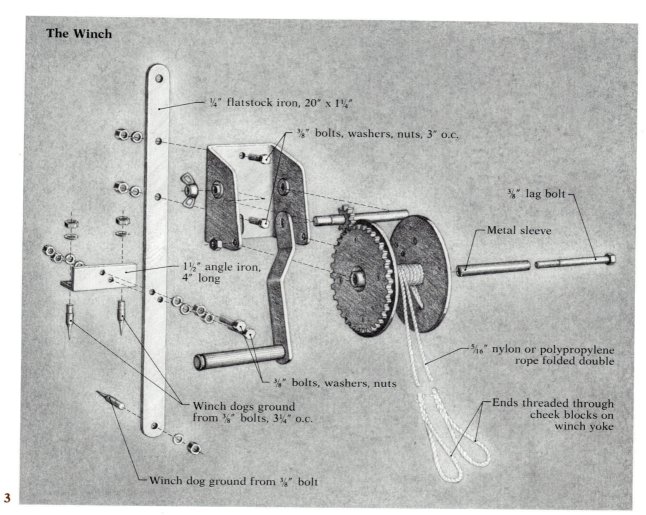

¼" flatstock iron, 20" x 1¼"

⅜" bolts, washers, nuts, 3" o.c.

⅜" lag bolt

Metal sleeve

1½" angle iron, 4" long

⅜" bolts, washers, nuts

Winch dogs ground from ⅜" bolts, 3¼" o.c.

⁵⁄₁₆" nylon or polypropylene rope folded double

Ends threaded through cheek blocks on winch yoke

Winch dog ground from ⅜" bolt

3

4

Throttle Attachment

Because the operator is at one end of the log and the saw at the other when milling with my system, you need to build a remote throttle attachment **(1)** to work the saw trigger. This one is designed for a Stihl 090, so if you're using a different engine, you might have to adapt a little. The illustration **(2)** shows the parts you'll need. The surgical tubing should be long enough (about 6 in. to 8 in.) to provide proper tension in the open-throttle position. You can substitute shock cord for surgical tubing, if you wish.

When you assemble the parts, lubricate the bolt between the two flat washers so the bearing surface can move freely. Adjust the bearing tension of the two flat washers with the first nut so the arm moves easily without wobbling, and lock it with the second nut.

Through the saw handle, drill and tap a ¼-in. thread **(3)** and mount the attachment **(4)** by screwing the bolt into the hole and locking it with a nut and washer. I'll explain how to use the remote throttle attachment on p.94.

In addition to holding the throttle open when in a cut, the remote throttle attachment also can be used as a locking throttle when hand-milling. Because the operator doesn't have to hold the throttle open manually, the amount of vibration normally endured is reduced. To use the attachment as a locking throttle, open the eye on the free end of the surgical tubing to form a hook, then drill a small hole in the engine casting to accommodate the hook **(5)**. A small piece of string tied around the ends of the surgical tubing will keep the eyes secure. Flip the attachment to an open position **(6)** for convenient hands-off, open-throttle milling.

1

The Throttle Attachment

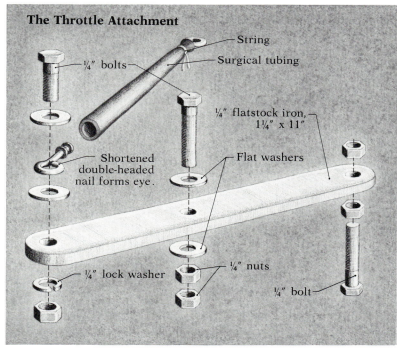

¼" bolts

String

Surgical tubing

¼" flatstock iron, 1¼" x 11"

Flat washers

Shortened double-headed nail forms eye.

¼" lock washer

¼" nuts

¼" bolt

2

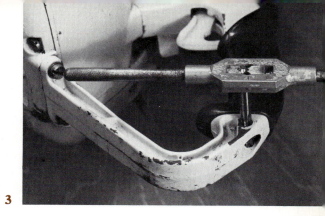

3

4

5

6

49

Saw Bridle Button

The winching rope is attached at one end to the mill (p. 42) and at the other end to the middle of a length of rope I call the bridle rope. One end of the bridle rope goes to the remote throttle attachment; the other end must attach to the saw. But since there's no place on the saw to accept a rope, you have to make a holding button. I call this the bridle button.

On the Stihl 090, I substitute a $\frac{5}{16}'' \times 1\frac{1}{2}''$ bolt for the original metric bolt (1) to make the bridle button. This is the logical place for it, as the bolt is in a strong position on the saw and in the line of pull when winching through a cut. If the threads on the bolt don't go all the way to the head, drill out the mating nut with a $\frac{5}{16}$-in. drill. Two $\frac{3}{8}$-in. flat washers hold the bridle rope around the nut (2). I prefer to use a star lock washer, mounted against the engine casting or under the bolthead, instead of a $\frac{5}{16}$-in. split lock washer, because it's easier on the aluminum. Torque the bolt assembly securely through the engine casting and into the bolt hole in the handle. The photo (3) shows how the bridle rope is mounted on the button.

The Winch Yoke

For the mill to be pulled at bar level in a straight path you need a winch yoke (4). The yoke also helps keep the guide rails of the mill level on the top plank. The cheek blocks on the ends of the yoke direct the rope slightly downward for a well-controlled cut (5).

1

3

2

5

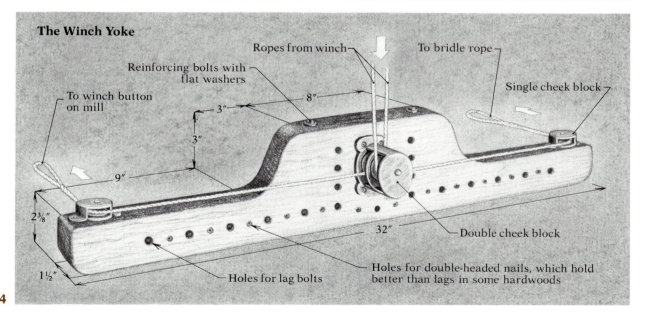

The Winch Yoke

Ropes from winch

Reinforcing bolts with
flat washers

To bridle rope

To winch button
on mill

Single cheek block

8″

3″

3″

9″

2⅜″

32″

Double cheek block

1½″

Holes for lag bolts

Holes for double-headed nails, which hold
better than lags in some hardwoods

4

Chapter 6

Lag Driver

To complete your milling kit, here are a few handy, work-saving tools that can easily be made from existing tools.

Using a box-end wrench or a ratchet-handled socket wrench to drive lag bolts (p. 86) is tedious work. I prefer to use a hand-drill brace and a modified short extension bar from a ⅜-in. or ½-in. socket set. Simply grind the square-holed end of the extension bar to fit the brace (1,2,3). Use a hexagonal (6-point) socket for hex-head lag bolts and an octagonal (8-point) socket for square-head lags (4).

If you want to make the modification permanent, weld the socket to a drill-brace collar (5). Keep the collar from turning by drilling and bolting it to the ratchet head with a ¼-in. or 5/16-in. bolt and nut. Secure the nut by riveting the bolt over it, or use a center punch to expand the bolt into the nut. Keep the moving parts of the brace well oiled.

1

2

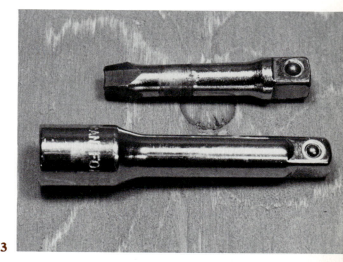

3

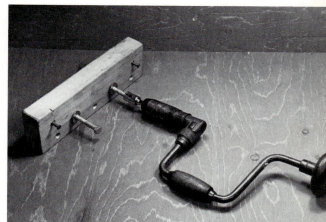

4

5

Build Your Own Tools

End Dogs

The inner tensions of a tree, caused by its reaction to the environment, often make boards twist or bend as soon as they're sawn. This distortion can throw off a properly aligned milling system. So I've designed end dogs to help keep boards straight until the cut is complete—the dogs tack board and log together, so the board can't deform during the cut.

The best end dogs can be forged from short pieces of automobile leaf spring (1), though other hardened steel would probably do as well. These end dogs are durable, easy to set and rarely need maintenance. To make them, first round the ends of the spring stock. Then heat and bend the ends so that they are at right angles to the flat stock. Reheat the dog to a dull red, and allow it to cool slowly in the air to harden. Grind the upturned ends from the outside to a sharp edge and then grind the edge straight across so that it is about $\frac{1}{32}$ in. to $\frac{1}{16}$ in. wide. End dogs with edges that are too sharp deform eventually and become difficult to drive.

If you don't have access to a forge, you can make adequate end dogs from square steel, aluminum tube or even flatstock iron (2,3). You can also modify an extra set of thrust skids (4,5). Simply drill holes to accommodate lag bolts. Use $\frac{3}{8}$-in.-diameter lags or, for the convenience of using the same lag driver, use lags of the same diameter as those used for guide-plank supports.

1

2

4

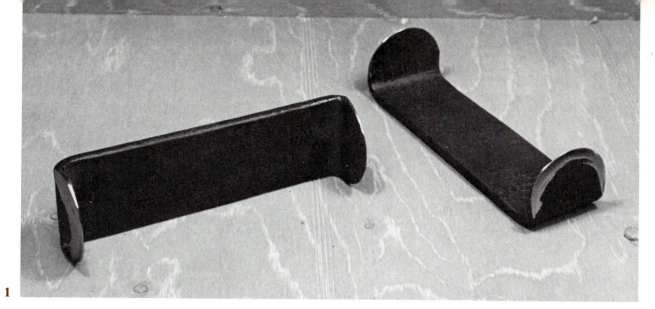

3

5

Kerf Wedges

As a saw moves through wood, the width of the cut it makes is called a kerf. In milling, the piece being sawn tends to sag into the kerf as the saw opens up the log. This often causes the chain to pinch. Sagging also causes an uneven cut, because the flat surface on which the mill's guide rails ride becomes unparallel to the desired cutting line. At the end of a cut, the entire weight of the milled piece is carried by the bar. This causes the saw to make a deeper cut, which results in curved ends on the milled board.

To eliminate these problems, I insert kerf wedges every few feet of the cut. The wedges support the piece being milled and keep the kerf open, allowing the bar to travel freely. I also insert a wedge on each side of the log just before the end of the cut. This allows the mill to exit easily and eliminates end run-off. Six or eight wedges are sufficient for most milling jobs.

Make the wedges from pieces of hardwood that are about $\frac{1}{32}$ in. thicker than the kerf (1). Taper the ends of the wedges slightly and round the corners for easy entrance into the kerf. Rounded handle ends with chamfered edges are easy on the hands. I paint my wedges a bright color to make them easy to spot if they drop into the sawdust. The paint helps preserve the wood, too.

Jacks

One or two bumper jacks are invaluable tools for rolling or lifting large logs or cants, and for clamping wood into various positions. But the base of an unmodified jack tends to slip off its footing or sink into the ground (2). To overcome this problem, I use two $\frac{3}{8}$-in. bolts and nuts as holding dogs. Bolted to the base, they grip rocky surfaces or bite into crosspieces placed underneath the jack.

To prevent the jack from slipping at the point of contact with the log, it's necessary to weld a dog securely to the jaw of the jack (3). Cut the dog from a piece of flatstock iron and grind one end to a sloping edge for good bite and easy release. Keep the moving parts of your jack well lubricated with chain oil.

1

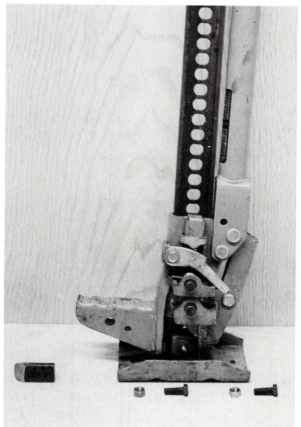

2

3

IN THE FIELD

Chapter 7

Safety and Tools

Felling a tree is the most dangerous part of lumbermaking. To do it well is an art—fell only when you fully understand the process and hazards, and are sure you can handle the work safely. I have felled trees professionally for over 25 years and am alive and well today only because of my dedication to safety.

Safe felling requires strict working habits. When I first broke in as a feller, an old-time logger told me, "Watch out for your tools, they're out to get you." I respected his advice, and it has kept me alive long enough to learn that it isn't always the tool that's out to get you—you can also get yourself. But with well-maintained tools, you certainly have less chance of getting hurt. So always keep your ax sharp, its handle tight and your chainsaw well serviced.

In the field, always wear a hardhat and safety glasses. Loose clothing can easily get caught in a running saw, so wear only well-fitting clothing and boots. It's also a good idea to wear hearing protection, even for short work periods, because the noise of a roaring chainsaw can damage, or even destroy, your hearing. I started felling trees long before ear protection was common in the woods and have become accustomed to listening for the warning sounds of falling limbs and breaking trees, so sometimes I choose not to wear hearing protection.

Never become overconfident when felling, and never cut down a tree when you are hampered by wind or bad weather. Stay away from alcohol and drugs, and don't work when you are tired. Fatigue can cause you to work dangerously—a hot chainsaw muffler can cause a serious burn; a slip of a wrench and you could cut your hand on the chain. Also, try not to work alone, but if you must, at least tell someone when and where you're going and when you will return. Always keep a well-equipped first-aid kit nearby. If you have assistants, never assume they understand work dangers: It's up to you to insist upon safety.

In short, don't take risks. Every time I step up to a tree that I want to fell, I feel a tingle of fear run down my spine. Don't feel embarrassed if you'd rather not take on this aspect of lumbermaking. There are experienced professionals who can do the job for you.

Because this book is about lumbermaking, I won't try to cover all the details of the felling process, but I will recommend an excellent book that does. The *Faller's and Bucker's Handbook*, published by the Worker's Compensation Board of British Columbia (5225 Heather St., Vancouver, B.C., Canada V5Z 3L8), is a modestly priced, logging-industry handbook that I find quite helpful.

The felling tools you will need will vary with your situation and skills. Here is a basic list:
- a saw engine coupled to a bar equipped with crosscutting chain
- a file for sharpening chain
- a bar wrench
- a measuring tape
- safety gear
- engine fuel and oil
- a properly serviced ax
  A single-bit, 3½-lb. ax is good for felling and wedge driving. Check that the axhead is on tight, and round off the sharp edges on the back of the head to reduce wedge wear. I usually store my working axhead in water, especially in hot, dry weather, to keep the wood from loosening around the head. Always keep your ax in a safe and handy position for easy access during felling.
- two or more felling wedges
  These wedges are different from splitting wedges. You can make them from hardwood, but I usually buy the plastic ones sold by chainsaw-supply dealers because they are more durable. Never use steel wedges with a chainsaw because one slip can wipe out the chain cutters. Experiment with wedges of various lengths and thicknesses, as different timber and weather conditions require different designs. Frozen wood, for example, requires special wedges.

Keep tools and fuel in a convenient cache behind a stump or standing tree, safe from falling limbs or a misdirected tree.

Felling a Tree

Tree Selection

The usefulness of the lumber you mill in part depends on the tree species, so proper identification is crucial. Develop a working knowledge of the types of trees in your area, and learn to identify each one **(1)**.

Tree structure will also help determine usefulness—consider the number of limbs on the tree (and the number of knots hidden within). Does the tree twist? If so, the grain of the wood most likely will twist, too. Does the tree lean? Leaning trees contain reaction wood, which moves and machines abnormally.

Also consider tree size. Measure the tree's diameter to be sure your mill can handle it **(2)**.

Once you've selected a tree, see if it can be felled to a good working location. Will it leave damaged limbs on adjacent trees that could threaten your safety during milling? Does the tree have a dead top or broken limbs? Is its butt hollow or decayed? Test for soundness by thumping the tree around its base with your axhead **(3)**. An unsound butt could cause a tree to fall to an unsafe or inconvenient milling site or to hang up in an adjacent tree.

1

2

3

Site Preparation

Clear away any limbs, brush, roots, stumps and rocks from around the base of the tree you've chosen, and select a convenient site for debris. Then remove all tree limbs as high as your saw can reach, cutting them as close to the tree as possible **(1)**. Make sure your saw is getting plenty of lubrication, and until you know that it is, try not to run the chain too fast, especially on automatic-oiling saws. With a saw having a manual oiler, pump it to get lots of oil on the bar and chain.

Check the base of the tree trunk for obstructions such as spikes, wire fence and rock, and remove any with an ax. Then establish the line of fall. A straight tree can usually be directed to the desired location easily, but if the tree leans, you must take corrective steps.

To determine a tree's lean, hold your ax up to the tree with the blade edge at the center of the trunk. Sight up the handle **(2)**. Repeat in two or three other locations for an accurate reading. If the tree leans away from the proposed line of fall, wedges driven into the back-cut (p. 66) can lift the tree past its center of gravity toward the desired location.

Now clear at least two escape paths away from the proposed line of fall and at least one path in the line of fall, in case wind, overcutting or other errors cause the tree to fall in the opposite direction. Select a stout tree or stump at the end of each path as shelter from flying limbs and treetops.

Bedding logs **(3)** placed across the proposed line of fall will support the tree at a convenient height and protect it from dirt and rocks. Determine the lengths of the logs you intend to buck from the tree, and place bedding logs at intervals relative to these. Bedding logs should be long enough to compensate for errors in felling direction and thick enough to support the tree. Be careful not to use thin logs, which might break on impact, but on the other hand, don't use logs that are too thick—these can cause the tree to break when it is felled across them.

Some trees are too brittle for this approach. Lift brittle logs to a convenient milling height after the tree is felled and bucked to length.

1

2

3

Felling the Tree

There are three cuts necessary to fell a tree: the first undercut, the second undercut and the backcut. While cutting, try not to stand under the lean of the tree.

With the chain well lubricated, start the undercut with the felling spikes of the saw up against the tree (1). Cut into the tree a distance between a quarter and halfway, keeping the cut level (2). Then remove the saw.

The second undercut meets the first to form a wedge that is later removed, allowing the tree to hinge down on the remaining wood (3). Start the second undercut above the first, at an angle that will allow it to meet the end of the first cut. The height of this cut should be at least a third of the first cut's depth—too narrow a wedge will cause the tree to break the hinge prematurely. Make sure the two cuts meet exactly on each side of the wedge opening; if the second undercut slants to one side, the tree will hinge down on the narrower side first, and swing in that direction. After you complete the cut, remove the wedge with your ax if necessary.

Now place the head of your ax into the undercut (4) so that its handle is at a right angle to the line of the cut; the handle will point to the direction of fall (5). Reposition bedding logs if you have to. Remove the ax and start the backcut opposite to and a little above the first undercut (6). Keep the backcut level.

1

2

3

4

5

6

With the saw into the cut enough to allow you to drive in a wedge, but not enough to start the tree moving, set a wedge at the center of the tree **(1)**, being careful not to hit the chain. The wedge will support the tree during the remainder of the cut; if the tree doesn't fall when the cut is finished, drive the wedge in further to lift the tree and start the fall. When driving a wedge, short blows work better than long, hard drives. Always break up the frequency of wedge pounding, however, as regular rhythm can set up enough vibration in a tree to cause a brittle treetop or limb to break off and hit you on the head.

Continue the backcut **(2)**, stopping when the bar gets close to the undercut. Don't cut all the way through the tree—leave enough wood for the tree to hinge upon. Too little holding wood will cause the tree to slip or twist off the stump, and the tree won't fall in the expected direction. Experience will teach you how much hinge to leave.

The tree will usually begin to fall before the backcut is finished **(3)**. Stop the saw and put it in a safe place as you retreat. Or take it with you as you wait in safety for the tree to hit the ground. Before you move again, check for widow-makers—limbs that might be hung up in nearby trees and have yet to fall. Take your time and be certain it's safe to continue.

Carefully examine the felled tree to be sure it has settled safely on the ground. Sometimes you'll have to cut limbs off the felled tree to complete the fall. Buck off the butt section if you think it's necessary **(4)**. Remove all broken limbs on adjoining trees, even if it means having to fell another tree.

There are probably as many different felling situations as there are trees standing. These are simply the basic considerations. Learn safe felling practices, or have a professional feller do the job for you.

1

2

3

4

Limbing

I usually cut the limbs off each tree before felling the next one. This makes it easier to clear the milling site. But reposition the bedding logs where necessary **(1)** before removing any supporting limbs. Remember that the limbs may be under tension and can kick back at you or at the sawbar, which in turn can kick back at you. Sometimes it is best to relieve stress by cutting the limb in half before cutting it off **(2)**.

Begin to limb from the top side of the tree **(3)**, being careful to keep a safe footing at all times. Overcut and undercut the limbs with the nose of the sawbar.

As you near the final stages of removing the supporting limbs, be ready to move away quickly, for the tree can roll, swing or drop. Plan your moves in advance. I try to imagine where I would land, and where I'd toss the running saw, if I should stumble and fall.

After limbing, trim off any irregularities that may interfere with milling **(4)**.

1

2

4

3

Bucking

Once you've limbed the tree, buck it into logs. Measure and mark out the tree to the desired log lengths with a tape **(1)**, allowing enough length for end trimming and squaring. I usually mark off log lengths by axing straight down, then axing in at an angle **(2)**. This produces a chip that often stays attached to the log—helpful when viewing the whole tree. When marking is complete, reposition bedding logs as necessary **(3)**.

If the tree to be bucked is on a hill, try to buck it from the uphill side. Bucked logs can roll or swing, which is dangerous if you're in the line of movement.

Bucking requires at least a basic understanding of sawing problems, of which the main one is a pinched sawbar. Beaver-tailing, or boring with the nose of the bar, is a good way to deal with pinching. As you feel a pinch happening, pull the saw out of the cut. Then bore into the cut repeatedly to remove the wood that is closing in on the kerf. Be careful not to let the chain touch the ground at this point. Continue bucking when the top of the log has closed completely.

A technique to avoid pinching and also splitting, which is another problem in log bucking, is underbucking **(4)**. Start at the underside of the log and cut with the top of the bar until you feel a pinch, or until a good portion of the cut is completed. Lift the saw with your legs, not your back. Underbucking causes the saw to push toward the operator, so I usually use only enough bar to get through the log. When you've completed the undercut, start in from the top **(5)**. Be prepared for the log to drop, and free your saw accordingly. If this log had not been underbucked, it would have split, because its end was not resting either on a bedding log or on the ground.

1

2

3

4

5

Felling a Tree

If your saw does get pinched in a log, wedge, jack, or saw it out or chop it out with an ax. Remove the engine from the bar for safety.

After bucking the logs, position them so they allow plenty of working space. If you place the logs with their straightest sides up, it will be easier to mill them later.

A peavey is handy for rolling or swinging logs (1). Keep the peavey hook sharp enough for good log entry, but not so sharp that it will stick. Always pull with one leg in front of the other (2). You can get a stronger pull with both feet together, but if the hook lets go or the handle breaks while you are in this position, you can easily hurt yourself. If the logs are too heavy to roll, the modified jack (p. 56) comes in handy (3).

When the logs are in position, block each one to keep it from moving. Now is the ideal time to seal the log ends to retard checking. You can do this after the wood is milled and the lumber stacked, but I find it best to seal fresh-cut log ends, especially when milling high-grade lumber or working under very dry conditions. Lumber end-sealing wax is common to the milling industry. I use one manufactured by Mobil Oil Corp. (150 E. 42nd St., N.Y., N.Y. 10017), called Mobil-Cer M, which is sold in 55-gal. barrels. You could also use melted paraffin wax or house paint, but these aren't nearly as good.

Chapter 8

Equipment for the First Cut

Before you can begin to mill any lumber, you must establish a level surface on each log to guide the first cut. My system consists of a straight guide plank resting on end boards and pairs of leveled lag bolts placed along the length of the log (**1**). The guide plank should be at least as wide as a third the width of the cut to be made. The wider the plank, the more support for the mill. The plank should also be thick enough to support the weight of the mill with minimum help from the lag bolts.

Guide-plank lengths will vary according to the lengths of the logs being milled, but I find that a 10-ft.-long, dressed 2x12 works in most situations and can be easily moved from site to site. The guide plank needn't be as long as the log being milled, because you can mill in stages by sliding the plank off the end board and along the lag bolts as you go.

To stiffen the plank and help keep it straight, and to allow the plank to slide along the lag bolts without damage, attach two $\frac{3}{16}$-in., $1\frac{1}{2}$" x $1\frac{1}{2}$" angle irons to the plank edges, using countersunk screws about every 12 in. The inside edges of the angle irons should be in line with the outside edges of the plank (1). To retard checking and warping, I treat the plank with linseed oil periodically. This also helps the mill to slide along the plank.

The guide plank is supported at both ends of the log by end boards. I usually make pairs of end boards from common, 2-in.-thick, dressed lumber. Heights of 4 in., 6 in., 8 in. and 10 in., cut to the width of the guide plank being used, cover most milling situations (2). The maximum height of your end boards is determined by the maximum cutting height of your mill, less the thickness of the guide plank and angle iron. For example, the mill I use here has a maximum cutting height of 13 in., the guide plank is $1\frac{5}{8}$ in. thick and the angle iron is $\frac{3}{16}$ in. thick. Therefore, the tallest end board I could use would be a little over 11 in. Because I usually allow at least an inch of clearance for the bottom of the lag bolts that run along the length of the log, the tallest board I would use would be 10 in.

Drill holes for lag bolts or double-headed nails at a variety of positions on the bottom of the boards and file notches on the top of the face of each end board. Because the angle iron I use is $1\frac{1}{2}$ in. wide, each notch must be inset $1\frac{1}{2}$ in. from the end. These notches will aid you later, when you align the lag bolts to support the guide plank with a taut line of string. Set shortened, double-headed nails around which to wrap the string just below the notches.

It's best to use the shortest lag bolts possible to support the guide plank (and therefore the shortest possible end boards) because short lag bolts are more rigid and have less chance of binding as the plank slides over them for successive cuts.

Lag bolts are used for a number of purposes in milling, so I routinely stock about six to ten each of $\frac{3}{8}$-in.-diameter lags in lengths of 3 in. through 10 in. at 1-in. increments. A supply of $2\frac{1}{2}$-in. lags also comes in handy. I prefer $\frac{3}{8}$-in.-diameter lags because they're easier to drive; $\frac{1}{2}$-in. lags are sturdier, but much harder to drive unless holes are predrilled with a $\frac{7}{16}$-in. drill. Applying bar soap, paraffin wax, or chain oil to the threads makes all lags easier to drive.

1

2

Index Lines

To make square lumber from a round log, you must first establish reference points from which to calculate your milling patterns. You can either mill to the heart center (pith) of a log or to average center **(1)**. On relatively straight logs, milling to the heart center will allow you to retrieve a larger percentage of straight-grained boards than milling to average center. On logs with excessive taper, where the heart center is way off average center and parallel to the taper, you'll be able to retrieve a larger volume of boards by milling to average center rather than to the heart. But the result will be that a great number of the boards will have cross grain (grain that deviates from the long axis of the board), and therefore will be of lower grade. Also, a log formed this way is liable to contain reaction wood, which shrinks and machines abnormally.

Measuring the top end of this log **(2)** shows that the heart center is just slightly off average center. This is true of the butt of the log as well. With this log, grade as well as volume are possible, and I'll mill to the heart center.

Mark out the index lines by drawing a short vertical line through the heart center at the butt and top of the log **(3)**, and then a short horizontal mark on each **(4)**.

2

3

4

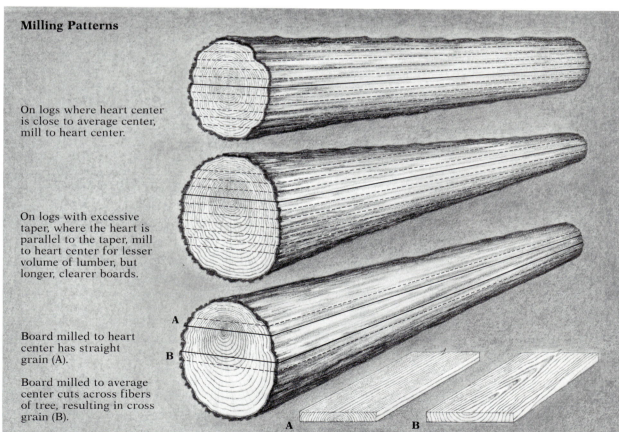

Milling Patterns

On logs where heart center is close to average center, mill to heart center.

On logs with excessive taper, where the heart is parallel to the taper, mill to heart center for lesser volume of lumber, but longer, clearer boards.

Board milled to heart center has straight grain (A).

Board milled to average center cuts across fibers of tree, resulting in cross grain (B).

A

B

A   B

1

Setting Up

Working at the top of the log, draw level horizontal and vertical lines end to end through the indexed heart **(1)**. Establish the width and height of the cant, and center it on the index lines **(2)**. From this 12-in. cant I will mill 2x12s, which I will later resaw into 2x8s and 2x4s.

Now go to the butt end of the log. The butt often has irregularities such as flare, which may need to be removed to accommodate the mill. Mark out the flare, then draw horizontal and vertical index lines. With a level, draw straight lines across the area to be removed **(3)**. Mark out cant lines as you did on the top end of the log **(4)**, then remove the flare with either crosscutting or ripping chain **(5)**.

1

2

3

4

5

Now decide which end boards to use. The idea here is that the top edges of the end boards will establish a plane parallel to the heart center of the log. This means that the top edges of the boards you bolt to either end of the log must be the same distance above the horizontal index lines **(1)**. At the same time, you want to use the shortest possible end boards that will still allow room for the lags to be bolted into the log. End boards that are too long will interfere with the first cut.

First go to the butt end of the log and measure from its top surface down to the junction of the index lines. Add enough height so the angle iron on the guide plank will clear the log, then lock your tape at this total. The end board at this end must reach up to this measurement, with enough overlap to be bolted into place. So must the taller board you'll need at the top end of the log.

When you've figured out the board sizes you'll need, position the top end board, hammer-start one of the lag bolts and screw it in with the lag driver. Then level the board and screw in the second lag **(2)**. Install the butt board in the same way.

Before installing the lag bolts that support the guide plank, attach a string to one of the nails on either end board and pass it through the notch **(3)**. Wrap the string around the nails on the other board **(4)**, bring it home and wrap it around the last nail. Pull it tight and secure it with a few wraps and a couple of half hitches **(5)**.

2

4

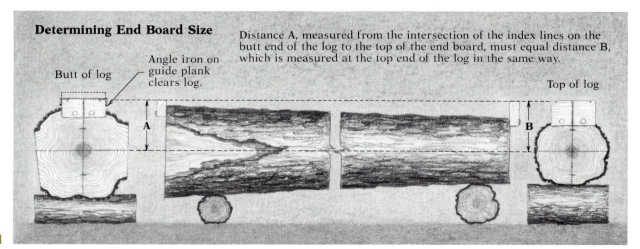

3

5

Determining End Board Size

Distance A, measured from the intersection of the index lines on the butt end of the log to the top of the end board, must equal distance B, which is measured at the top end of the log in the same way.

Butt of log

Angle iron on guide plank clears log.

A

B

Top of log

1

Measure and mark the log for the supporting lag bolts. When using a 10-ft. guide plank, I usually place a pair of lags every 4 ft. To select lags of proper length, measure from the bottom of the strings to the marked positions on the log (1), and then add on about 1½ in. for holding. Check the measurement in several places as the lengths required may vary. You may have to remove high spots on the log with a chainsaw or ax—drawing a string or measuring tape from one end of the log to the other will let you see any irregularities. Remember to make sure the lags don't go so deep that they're in the path of the cut.

Drive-start the bolts on the outside of the strings (no further than 1¼ in. away) at the marked positions (2), then screw them in so that the tops of the boltheads are the same height as the bottom of the string (3). Make sure the lags don't touch the strings. When all the bolts are in place, sight down the log to double-check alignment of the end boards, and remove the string.

Position the guide plank, looking under it to make sure the angle irons rest securely on the lags and end boards. You'll need an overhang of at least 12 in. to support the mill as it begins the cut, so pull the plank out (4).

If you're milling with a winch, you'll need a weight to hold the guide rails of the mill flat on the plank. Make this from a block of log that is slightly larger in diameter than the space between the mill guide rails. You'll have to notch out the log for the mill handle (5). Mark the notch with a crayon (6) and make a cut deep enough to give good handle clearance. Remove the wedge of wood with a second cut and, if you need it, a third (7). Then test the fit of the weight on the mill (8).

1

2

3

Setting Up

4

5

6

7

8

Changing the Bar

If you use one saw engine both for felling and lumbermaking, you will now need to remove the felling bar and crosscut chain. Before mounting the milling bar and mill, clean the cover plate and blade area of the saw engine with a stiff brush (1). Then unscrew the chain-tension screw to full slack position (2). Double-check for a clean oiler hole on the engine and the bar, and mount the bar and mill. Replace the chain-guide plate, making sure the tension stud is properly positioned. Tighten the bar nuts on the lubricated bolts with your fingers (3).

Now for the chain. Chain often gets tangled into what seems like a hopeless mess when it is moved around. To roll the kinks out, hold the chain in both hands. Starting with the most serious kink (4), roll the chain as shown (5). Pull the two loops into the final loop, and you're ready to mount the chain on the bar (6).

If you're not used to handling chain, it's a good idea to wear gloves because sharp cutters can seriously injure bare hands.

1

2

3

4

6

5

Chapter 9

The First Cut

Because all logs are shaped differently, the first cut must establish a level and flat working surface that will guide the rest of the milling. If the first cut is off, the other cuts will be off, too.

Determine how high to set the mill for the first cut by measuring from the top of the guide plank to the top cant mark on the vertical index line (1). For this log, I'll set my mill at 11 in. Start the saw, and pump out an excess of chain oil (2); remember to check the chain frequently for good lubrication.

Mount the mill on the guide plank. As you push the mill forward to begin the cut, press down firmly on its handle (3) to keep the guide rails level on the plank. Gently rev up the engine to full throttle as the saw starts to cut. Keep the thrust skids against the log and enter the cut with the nose end of the sawbar. Cut at full throttle until the back guide rail of the mill just passes the end board (4). Drive in both end dogs (5), spacing them as far apart as possible. But make sure not to pound the dogs so close to the edges of the cut that the top slab splits.

1

2

3

5

4

Now position the winch yoke. Center it on the butt end of the log so that the outside pulleys are 1 in. or 2 in. below the top cant mark on the vertical index line (**1**). Mount the yoke with washered lag bolts.

Drive the winch dogs into the top of the end board (**2**). It's sometimes best to predrill the end boards to keep the dogs from splitting the wood.

Thread one end of the winch rope through the double cheek block in the center of the winch and out to an end block (**3**). Thread the other end of the rope through to the remaining cheek block. You can remove the winch handle so that as you pull the ropes through the yoke (**4**), the winch will not vibrate off its mounting. If you don't want to bother doing this, just pull the ropes out a little more slowly.

1

2

3

4

When you're down at the mill end of the log, thread the outside rope around the spacer nuts and set its eye over the winch button **(1)**. Then put back the winch handle, if you removed it earlier, and winch this rope to a light but snug tension **(2)**.

Now slip one end of the bridle rope over the bridle button on the saw engine, and hook the other end of the bridle rope to the eye on the remote throttle attachment **(3)**. The length of the bridle rope should be about twice the distance between the bridle button and the throttle eye. Gently take up the slack in the winch rope **(4)**, and thread it through the bridle rope so that it will pull the throttle wide open before pulling the mill forward **(5)**. When you find the proper position, mark it with a piece of tape. Try various positions for a well-synchronized pull. As a guideline, the length of rope going to the bridle button should be shorter than the length of rope going to the throttle.

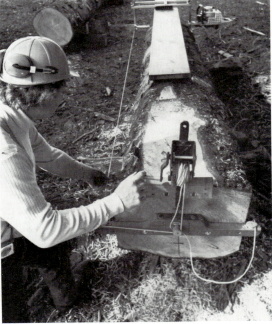

1

2

3

4

5

As various ropes knot differently, on ropes of unknown material I use a double sheet bend **(1)** for easy removal. On ropes I know, I usually use a single sheet bend with a loop **(2)**. I don't recommend using a metal hook instead of a knot, because the hook could whip back at you if the rope were to break.

The piece of tape that marks the position of the winch rope on the bridle rope will soon be pulled off. But the permanent kink the knot leaves in the rope will help you realign the next hookup for a synchronized pull **(3)**.

1

Sheet Bend

1.

2.

To tie a single sheet bend knot, make a bight (uncrossed loop) in the longer end of the bridle rope (1). Weave the winch rope through the eye, around the bight (2),

3.

4.

and back under itself (3). Snug the knot securely so that it won't slip when the rope is tensed (4).

2

3

When the winch is set up, start the saw engine and position the counterweight (1). As you start cranking the winch (2), the engine should open up to full throttle. (You shouldn't have to put heavy pressure on the winch handle.) You will soon learn to coordinate engine speed with winching speed. Check the tension of the winch lines occasionally—rope breakage can be dangerous, so watch out for it.

To keep the top slab from sagging and pinching the bar, stop milling and place kerf wedges on both sides of the cut as needed (3). The number of wedges and their placement will depend upon the weight of the slab. Wedging can be done by your partner, if you have one, but make sure he or she keeps both hands far away from the chain. To stop milling, or if the saw sticks in the cut, turn the winch handle backward quickly for several rotations. This will stop the pull and allow the engine to return to idle.

Keep an eye on the guide rails of the mill to be sure they remain flat on the guide plank, and mill up to the last set of lag bolts (4). Crank the winch backward quickly to stop milling, allow the engine to idle and then turn the engine off.

1

2

3

4

1

Remove the counterweight and winch, leaving the ropes attached to the engine. Pull the guide plank forward to the next cutting position (1). In the last position, the plank should just cover the end board (2). It's a good idea to check the lag bolts to make sure they haven't been bent. With this system you can cut any length of log, as long as you accurately set the end boards and lags.

2

Now set the winch dogs into the end of the guide plank (3), replace the counterweight and continue milling, adding kerf wedges as necessary (4). When the mill comes close to the end of the cut (5), remove the counterweight, winch ropes and yoke (6). A final set of kerf wedges will keep the top slab from dropping on the saw as the cut is completed (7).

3

4

6

5

7

Pull the guide plank forward (**1**) to support the mill as it finishes the cut. Complete the cut by hand, keeping a firm downward as well as a forward pressure on the mill (**2**). Reducing engine speed to idle as soon as the chain completes the cut lessens the chance of rounding over the edge, and of the chain scoring the board at the back of the bar. Stop the engine and set the mill aside. Remove kerf wedges and end dogs from the end of the log (**3**).

1

2

3

You can mill a board or two off the top slab if you invert it in place on top of the log. Estimate the center of weight of the slab and drive a plastic felling wedge on either side **(1)**. (The weight center is usually not the measured center of a log.) Absolute balance is not necessary, but the closer you guess, the easier it will be to move the slab.

Swing the slab with a peavey **(2)** so that it crosses the log. Use a peavey or jack to flip the slab over **(3)**. Swing the slab in place **(4)**, then lift it to near level and block it with a wedge **(5)**. (You can split wedges from the undercut wedge taken from the tree during felling.) For extra stability, wedge up the opposite end of the slab a little.

1

2

4

3

5

When I inspected the cut, I realized that I had a problem. New, modified ripping chain makes a surface that is close to planed, yet both sides of this cut were extremely rough. (You can see this in photo 1 on p. 109.) In a situation like this, the first thing to do is check chain tension, as this is the usual cause of a rough cut. A newly installed chain sometimes has kinks that loosen after the chain runs a while. A properly tensioned chain is easy to move around the bar by hand; pull it back and forth to test. Properly tensioned chain can also be lifted from the bar with normal finger pressure. This chain required abnormal pressure, so I realized it was too tight **(1)**.

If you stop for chain adjustment, it's a good idea to check the drive links for a film of oil. An oily buildup of sawdust on the nose end of the bar **(2)** is a good sign of proper lubrication.

After the first cut is also a good time to check the saw engine for fuel and chain oil. But before doing this, wipe sawdust away from the filling caps with a rag or stiff brush. Chain oil shouldn't be used up before fuel, as this will cause excessive bar and chain wear.

Try not to run out of fuel or chain oil before you complete a cut, unless you can add them both from the upper side of the engine. Otherwise, you'll have to back the mill out of the cut to fill up. After a few cuts, you'll learn to gauge fuel and oil consumption.

Here I'm adjusting the mill to cut a 2-in. board off the inverted top slab **(3)**. Riser posts that are free of pitch and dust allow you to raise and lower the guide-rail assembly easily. Doubling-up on the toggle adjustment nuts **(4)** will ensure that the cut stays straight.

1

3

2

4

To begin the cut, position the adjustable entry guide rail in the center of the slab **(1)**. This rail supports the mill during exit and entry. Start cutting with the nose end of the bar, keeping the guide rails flat on the slab.

Set end dogs **(2)**, or if you feel the top slab will not curl up or twist, insert kerf wedges. Set up the winch **(3)**, lifting up on the winch handle as you drive or hand-press the front dog into the slab.

1

2

3

I don't normally use the winch yoke on shallow cuts. I attach the winch rope to the bridle rope at the engine end as when using the yoke, but attach the nose-end rope by slipping the loop over the riser post (1).

Once the counterweight is in position, you can start milling, setting kerf wedges as necessary. Near the end of the cut, remove the counterweight and winch, and set the final wedges (2). Complete the cut by swinging off or milling straight off—use whatever works best for you to keep the final stages of the cut straight (3). Experiment with different handholds to find the most comfortable position (4).

Now gently take off the slabbed board (5). The top slab of the log makes a good base for stacking your wood as you continue to work. Place it on the ground, support logs or level timbers. For air-drying, I use 1-in.-square stickers, but sticker size depends on how fast you want the wood to dry. The larger the sticker, the more air that circulates, and the faster the wood dries. Swing the slabbed board onto the stickered top slab (6).

1

2

3

4

5

6

2x12s

Now we'll mill 2x12s. Begin by adjusting the mill to cant width (12 in.). If you intend to re-saw the 2x12s into 2x4s and 2x8s (p. 126), adjust the mill to cant width plus saw kerf (here ⅜ in.) **(1)**. Kerf width varies with types of chain and narrows as the chain is ground or filed back. Measure for kerf width just behind the sawbar when the saw is stopped in a cut.

Start to mill, setting the end dogs after the mill is well into the cut **(2)**. Set up the winch, mount the counterweight and continue milling **(3)**. If your mill has square guide rails, they will scrape away the sawdust, but if your mill has roller guide rails, you'll constantly have to sweep away the sawdust ahead of them. Otherwise, the rollers will ride up on the sawdust, resulting in an irregular cut.

Insert kerf wedges as necessary and continue milling to the end of the cut. Then remove the winch and, after inserting the final two kerf wedges, complete the cut by hand-milling, as before **(4)**. Check the cut for accuracy **(5)**.

1

2

3

5

4

Before attempting to stand the cant on edge, you may have to support it for more convenient milling by placing additional bedding logs underneath **(1)**. Turn the cant (p. 104), driving two felling wedges into the cut at the estimated weight center, then swinging the cant with a peavey **(2)**. Lift and swing the cant with the peavey **(3)** or a modified jack, then block the cant upright in a stable position, using small blocks and wedges **(4)**. Once again, the rough cut shows me the chain needs to be retensioned (p. 44). Here is another good tool for turning a cant **(5)**.

Now draw a string or tape from one end of the cant to the other, to check for high spots. Remove them with an ax or chainsaw, so that you'll be able to use the shortest possible lag bolts to support the guide plank.

1

2

3

4

5

115

After the cant is turned, select and position the end boards (p. 84) **(1)**. Screw in one bolt, then square the board **(2)** and screw in the second bolt. Double-check to be certain you didn't disturb the square when screwing in the second bolt.

Attach the string to the end boards, pulling it taut. Mark and set lag bolts of proper length level to the bottom of the string, being careful not to select lags that will protrude into the milling area—the length of the longest lag bolt plus the thickness of the guide plank and angle iron must be less than the mill height setting. Sight down the lag bolts to double-check level, then remove the string.

Next, mount the guide plank on an end board and the lags **(3)**, checking that the plank is supported properly. Measure and mark the desired cut from the horizontal index line **(4)**, in this case, 6 in. Now measure from the top of the guide plank to that mark, and adjust your mill to this measurement. Measure and mark the other end of the log. This double-checks all previous calculations, shows the exit line of the saw and helps in positioning the winch yoke.

1

2

3

4

Start the cut with the guide rails flat on the plank and the thrust skid against the side of the cant (1). Set the end dogs, mount the winch apparatus (2) and counterweight, and mill (3,4).

When you're finished, turn the slab, swinging it across the cant, using felling wedges at the point of balance if necessary (5). Roll the slab over and swing it back onto the cant. Block as necessary to steady for milling.

From this slab we will mill one 2″ x 12⅜″ board. Adjust the mill for a 2-in. cut and move the entry guide rail to the center of the board to support the mill (6). Mill by hand until the saw is well into the cut. Set kerf wedges instead of dogs if you feel the board won't curl up too much (7). Then mount the counterweight and winch, and continue milling (8).

1

2

3

4

6

5

7

8

Notice how the winch rope, when used without the yoke on shallow cuts, spools unevenly **(1)**. To overcome uneven spooling, I replaced the short bolts on the winch with long ones **(2)** to act as fairleads and help even out the spooling. Improvement of milling equipment is an ongoing event, and as you read this book, you'll probably find many ways to improve your equipment and the art of milling. This simple modification certainly solved my problem.

While we're on the subject, here is another winch refinement. An adjustable winch coupler, made of a short cord with knotted ends **(3)**, allows milling closer to the winch at the end of the cut. This can replace the former cross-over system (shown in photo 1). Wrap the coupler around the winch ropes a few times and tie it with a square knot **(4)** or three or four half-hitches. Then attach the winch rope to the riser post for a direct pull **(5)**.

When you're at the end of the cut, remove the winch and counterweight, insert final kerf wedges, and hand-mill out of the cut **(6)**.

1

2

3

4

5

6

1

Swing off the board (**1**), and mill all usable lumber from the top slab (**2,3**). Swing the boards onto a pile convenient for milling into 2x4s and 2x8s (**4**). Continue sawing 2-in. boards for 2x12s or change the mill setting for boards of different thickness.

Eventually, the problem of the mill cutting too close to the bedding logs will arise. Solve this by elevating the cant with log supports. To make them, cut two log blocks and mark out a centerline on each. Then mark two parallel lines equidistant from the center line (**5**). This is one of the times an extra chainsaw comes in handy, and its bar makes a convenient straightedge and width gauge. Using the marked lines as guides, saw out notches (**6**). While you can do this freehand, you will probably get better results using lines.

2

3

4

5

6

Position the notched blocks beside the remainder of the cant (**1**), and swing one end at a time (**2**), lifting with your legs and not your back. If the cant is too heavy to move manually, use jacks or other equipment. Then you're ready to continue milling (**3**). I find it easier to stack lumber by swinging each end, rather than lifting the whole board at one time (**4**).

Readjust the mill to take a shallow last cut (**5**). Very thin boards can be milled quite accurately, but be sure to allow extra thickness for final dressing.

Hand-milling is much less complicated than the winch system, but certainly more tedious. I often hand-mill short and narrow cuts, but find a day's work much easier with a winch.

Swing and stack the final board from the remainder of the cant. Now you have a fine pile of 2x12s (**6**).

1

2

3

5

4

6

2x4s and 2x8s

If you want 2x4s and 2x8s, you can resaw your 2x12s. First measure the combined width of the boards to be resawn (1). As you will be stacking these boards on edge, you will need a base at least as wide as the combined width of the boards. Use the widest slab (2) for a base, extending its width with crossboards if necessary.

Arrange narrow and bark-edged boards in the center of the stack (3) and complete the assembly with a heavy, clear-edged board on each side. Use the modified jack or other device to clamp the boards together securely (4). Position the jack below the proposed cutting line (in this case, the cutting line is 4 in. from the top of the stack). Pound the board tops to level, if necessary, as you clamp the stack together (5), then check with a square.

1

2

3

4

5

Now adjust the mill to a cutting height of 4 in. and position the entry guide rail so it will ride on a board in the center of the stack. Start resawing (1). Insert kerf wedges when the mill is well into the cut (2), and attach the winching apparatus and counterweight (3). You won't need the yoke for shallow cuts.

After milling, double-check for accuracy. Notice how the $\frac{3}{8}$-in. kerf allowance on the 2x12s lets you saw perfect 4-in. and 8-in. boards (4). Restack the boards for air-drying, using stickers between them (5). The remaining slab (6) makes a good weight.

1

2

3

4

5

6

Chapter 10

Box-Heart Timber

Begin to mill a 12x12 box-heart timber by drawing vertical and horizontal index lines through the heart center at the top and butt of the log (**1**). Then center the timber on the index lines (**2,3**). Select your end boards: The top measurement of this log was 2 in. less than the butt, so I selected a 6-in. board for the butt end and an 8-in. board for the top. The 6-in. board allowed adequate angle-iron clearance; the 8-in. board took up the 2-in. taper.

Install and level the end boards (**4**), set the string and mark for the supporting lags. Check the length of the lags you select to make sure they won't be in the path of the first cut (**5**). Install the bolts to string level, sight for alignment (**6**), then remove the string.

1

2

3

4

5

6

131

Position the guide plank, checking to see that the angle irons rest securely on the end board and lag bolts. Set mill height **(1)**, then pull the guide plank out to start the cut and begin milling. Set the end dogs, mount the counterweight and winching unit **(2)**, and mill to the end of the guide plank, adding kerf wedges as necessary. Slide the plank to the next position and finish milling.

Remove the kerf wedges and end dogs and flip the slab to inspect the cut **(3)**. If you want to, you can make unedged lumber from this slab.

1

3

2

Now turn the log so that its straightest side is on top and the milled surface is approximately vertical (**1**). Block the log to prevent it from rolling over. Set up this surface for milling, making sure that you bolt the end boards square to the slabbed side of the log (**2**). Mill (**3,4,5,6,7**), then remove the slab (**8**).

1

2

3

4

5

6

7

8

For the third cut, adjust your mill to the bottom line. Hold the forward guide rail down firmly as you enter the cut for an accurate start **(1)**. Before you start a down and forward push, you can change your hand to a more comfortable position. Mill the cant **(2)**, adding kerf wedges as necessary. You can mill through support blocks as long as their actual point of support is below the cutting line **(3)**, but watch out in case the sawbar pinches or the log starts to roll.

1

2

3

When the cut is complete, pull the cant off the bottom slab and onto the bedding logs **(1)**, and move the bottom slab out of the way. Roll the cant barkside down and block it **(2)**. The mill setting remains the same for this next cut. Note the smooth cutting surface that results from sharp, properly tensioned ripping chain **(3)**.

When milling is done, roll the timber off the bottom slab. From this timber **(4)**, it is possible to make edge-grain (quartersawn) lumber by milling the timber into quarters along the index lines, then milling each quarter as shown **(5)**. But quartersawing like this isn't efficient, because to get a worthwhile amount of edge-grain lumber, you have to start with large logs. I prefer the system described in the next section.

1

2

3

Milling Quartersawn Lumber

5th cut

3rd cut

1st cut

6th cut →

4th cut →

2nd cut →

4

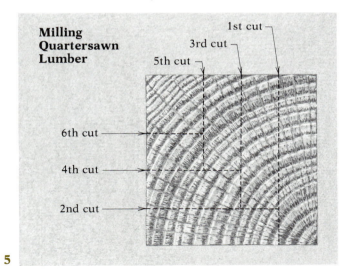

5

139

Quartersawn Lumber

My quartersawing system requires an extra edging process, but yields the maximum amount of quartersawn lumber. Start by drawing vertical and horizontal index lines through the heart of the log at the top and butt **(1)**. Mount the end boards in the usual manner. If you are milling a short log and feel the guide plank will not sag between end boards, skip the supporting lags.

Now measure from the top of the guide plank to the center of the horizontal index line. Subtract half the width of the saw kerf from this measurement and set your mill to the new measurement. If you don't subtract half the kerf width, the saw will cut below the center of the line. Double-check that the mill is set correctly by measuring the distance from the center of the chain drive links or bar groove to the bottom of the guide rail **(2)**.

Slide the guide plank out for mill entry and begin the cut **(3)**. If you want to save the time it takes to mount the winch and its accessories, mill by hand. But if you do, you'll have to endure engine noise, exhaust and sawdust, as well as the strain of holding the mill down while moving it along. It's your choice.

1

3

2

When the first cut is completed, set an end dog on each end of the halved log, to one side of the vertical index line **(1)**. Roll the log over to the second cutting position, and block or wedge it securely in place **(2)**. Mount end boards square to the vertical line **(3)**, and install lags for support if necessary. Then mount the guide plank. Measure from the top of the plank to the center of the horizontal line and again subtract half the kerf width **(4)**. Adjust the mill, double-checking to make sure the measurement is correct. As you become experienced in making a good starting cut, you won't need to overhang the guide plank **(5)**.

You'll end up with quartered cants **(6)**. A true heart cut will give you the pith of the log **(7)**, which can be removed by edging with a homemade edger (pp. 180-182), bandsaw, table saw, Skilsaw or radial-arm saw.

2

1

3

4

6

5

7

Now set one of the cants aside, and block the other in position for milling **(1)**. Short, double-headed spikes **(2)**, driven along the edge of the cutting platform, keep the cant from moving. Adjust the mill to cut at the desired thickness and start to mill in a progression of alternate sides **(3)**.

Occasionally, you may have to mill the same side two or more times to increase the number of longer, edge-grain boards **(4)**. This is often necessary when the heart center of the log is well off average center.

1

2

3

Quartersawing

Wood is usually quartersawn in a progression of alternate sides, but sometimes milling the same side two or more times will result in a greater number of longer, edge-grain boards.

2nd cut — 1st cut —
3rd cut —
4th cut —
5th cut —
6th cut —

4

Slabsawn Lumber

One of the simplest forms of chainsaw lumbermaking is straight slabbing. The boards are left unedged and are easily stacked and stickered for air-drying. The yield is a full assortment of flat-grain and edge-grain cuts.

Proceed using the milling methods described in Chapter 9. When you've milled the top slab, remove it and position it flat side up as a base for stacking (1). Place two or more stickers on the base (2). I usually use 1-in.-square stickers, but it's a good idea to look into systems used by local sawmills and lumberyards.

Now mill the rest of the slabs (3), allowing a little extra thickness on each for planing and sanding. A good stack of lumber and the satisfaction of a job well done are the results (4).

1

2

3

SPECIALTY MILLING

Chapter 11

Burls

The techniques I've just explained don't limit you to milling only standard lumber. With different end-board and guide-plank setups, you can easily mill lumber to special shapes and with exotic grain patterns. Milling burls, for example, is one of the most delightful and exciting lumbermaking experiences. Burls are abnormal outgrowths of trees, and the unusual wood found in them can be used dramatically in decorator slabs and furniture.

When you take a saw to a burl **(1)**, be especially cautious, for although burls can reveal real treasures, they are notorious for hiding rocks, sand and dirt—all hard on a chain. Take several sharp chains to your site to ensure a good day's productivity.

After bucking the burl to length, position it to a convenient height and stabilize it for milling. Measure its widest part **(2)** to make sure your mill can handle it.

In milling burls, as in milling logs, you need a flat top surface from which to mill the wood. For a guide plank, use any straight board that is at least a third the width of the burl and strong enough to support the mill. With an ax or a chainsaw, establish three points on the burl that will support the plank parallel to the cut you want to make **(3)**. Then tack the plank at those points with short nails **(4)**.

1

2

3

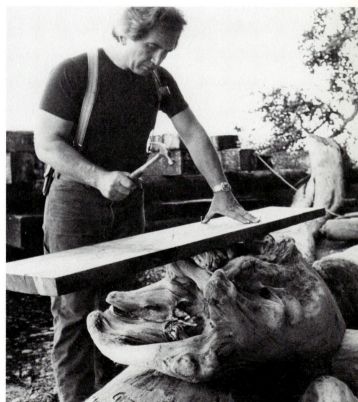

4

151

Measure from the top of the plank to various points along both sides of the burl to determine a cutting height out of the path of ingrown rocks **(1)**. Adjust the mill and begin cutting cautiously **(2)**, so as not to damage the chain severely if you strike a hidden rock. Insert kerf wedges as necessary. Remove the top slab **(3)** and pry it from the plank, removing the nails.

For the next cut, again examine the outside edges of the burl to determine a safe cutting level **(4)**. Don't forget to add in the thickness of the guide plank when setting mill height. Tack the plank to the burl and mill through the cut, using kerf wedges as needed **(5)**. Remove the slab from the plank. Notice the internal cavities that I've uncovered here **(6)**; these often house rocks and other abrasive materials.

1

2

3

4

6

5

153

Ovals

To mill oval slabs, I use a modified end-board system. I usually prop up the log securely with a notched support and then mount a short end board to level at the upper end of the log. At the lower end, I mount a longer board to level (1). These boards support the guide plank—tack it to the short end board with a couple of small nails (2), but leave the other end untacked to allow for mill exit.

Measure from the top of the plank to the desired cut to calculate the mill setting (3), then make the first cut (4,5,6).

1

2

3

5

4

6

Remove the milling accessories (**1**). You now have a level surface from which to saw the remainder of the log. Adjust the mill to the desired height and make the next cut (**2**). The entry guide rail of the mill is especially important here for support (**3**); keep it flat on the slab for a straight cut. As you continue milling, you'll eventually have to block the log in a stable position (**4**).

Here are the results (**5**).

3

1

2

4

5

Natural Knees

Building wooden boats requires special types and cuts of wood that are often expensive and difficult, if not impossible, to find. Making my own boat lumber frees me from the frustration of endless prowls through lumberyards and adds another dimension to the boatbuilding process: a boat from a tree.

The Lunenberg dory is my true love. For the dory in this photograph (1), which I modified from traditional East Coast design to meet my needs on the West Coast, I used the following materials:

- quartersawn red cedar for the lapstrake planking, thwarts and first bottom;
- yew for the natural-knee bow stem, stern, floor cleats and rub rails;
- flatsawn Douglas fir for the second bottom and second garboard strake;
- quartersawn Sitka spruce for oars;
- Douglas fir for the ribs (natural knees). The natural-knee ribs in this dory are much stronger than ribs made by joining.

Knees are usually found in heavy, spreading roots, but they may also be found in bent limbs, forked trunks and the curved butts of trees growing on the sides of hills (2). The strength of a knee depends on the type of wood and its soundness. On logs having no bark or leaves, I use a single-bit ax to slice away a little wood to identify the species by sight and smell. A few thumps with an ax-head help determine soundness. Knee wood should be free of pitch seams, rot and knots. Boatbuilding manuals and local boatbuilders can be a good source of information when you're deciding which trees in your area are right to use.

After bringing down your tree and bucking it to length, nail or bolt end boards at log top and butt (3). For strong knees with minimal cross-grain, the tops of the end boards on both ends of the log should be the same distance from the heart center.

1

2

3

Now stretch a line across the tops of the end boards and drive a lag bolt or nail at the center of the curve, level with the bottom of the string **(1)**. Drive a second lag to the level of the first **(2)**, spacing the lags at a distance less than the width of the guide plank you'll be using. Then remove the string.

Lay the guide plank over the top of one end board and both lag bolts and measure the distance from the heart center of the log to the top of the guide plank **(3)**. Adjust the mill to this measurement, set its entry guide rail to the center of the plank and mill **(4)**. Knees milled to each side of the pith will be close to quartersawn, which are the best for boat ribs.

Mill until the saw is well into the cut, and set the end dogs. When you reach the center of the curve, slide the guide plank to the other end board **(5)**, insert the kerf wedges and continue milling. Insert another pair of kerf wedges before the saw completes the cut. Remove the guide plank and the end boards.

1

4

2

3

5

Now flip the top slab and inspect it for a usable knee (**1**). Wedge or block the slab in a stable position (**2**) and adjust mill height to desired knee thickness. Start the cut and insert kerf wedges or set end dogs as necessary. Mill past the center of the curve and insert another pair of wedges (**3**). Insert a final pair of wedges before completing the cut (**4**). Repeat the process on the other slab for a second knee.

1

2

3

4

An alternative knee-milling system is especially useful on logs with sharp curves. Buck the selected log to length **(1)**, block it to a convenient height and draw a line through the heart centers on both of its ends **(2)**. Spike or bolt long end boards of equal height and width to the log. The tops of the boards should be higher than the top surface of the log; the bottoms should be placed on or equidistant from the heart lines **(3)**. Make sure the boards are level.

Mount a guide plank on the end boards. For box-heart natural knees, measure from the top of the guide plank to a point below the centerline that is half the thickness of the knee you want **(4)**. Set your mill to this measurement.

1

2

3

4

To start the cut, pass the mill over the guide plank and around the end board (**1**). Start to mill, setting end dogs or kerf wedges as necessary (**2**). Mill until you need to reposition the guide plank. Do this and complete the cut (**3**). Remove the top slab and flip it, adjust the mill to the desired knee thickness and mill (**4,5**).

1

2

3

4

5

167

Big Wood

In my opinion, most conventional forest harvesting techniques are detrimental to the forest and the land that supports our woods. Clear cutting and the use of heavy equipment often permanently alter existing ecosystems, whereas logging with a chainsaw, because it is a selective process, does not. With a chainsaw, the logger decides what to harvest—trees that are mature, damaged or crowding other trees. A tree is felled and milled where it falls. Only usable lumber is removed, leaving the byproducts to feed the land. And removing the milled lumber from the woods can be done with minimal disturbance.

Techniques for milling big wood (1) do not vary from those used to mill trees of average size. Procedures such as bucking, however, do require special consideration. A pinched bar in a big log can be extremely hard to free and the chances of a severely damaged bar and chain are high for the inexperienced bucker.

1

Special Cuts

Safety is a major consideration. It is especially important to think about your posture and footing when working with big wood. In this photograph **(1)**, I am shown standing a little to the side of the saw—comfortable and well balanced. If the saw needs to be removed quickly or if the log should move, I am in a good position to react. Remember, if you have to move suddenly, keep the bar and chain away from your legs.

I position big logs using two modified jacks. Once the first jack is set at the maximum safe height, set the second jack **(2)**. Alternately set and remove the jacks until the log is the way you want it. A block, in front of the third workman's foot in this photo, is used to prevent the log from rolling back.

You can mill big wood efficiently with a 4-ft. mill, but mills this large should be either custom-built or modified as discussed on p. 38. Even so, large mills can be trouble. Because the riser posts are far apart, they give only minimal support to the sawbar and bar sag becomes a real problem. And it's also difficult to generate sufficient power when using a large mill. Using two saw engines on one mill isn't the answer as it's just about impossible to synchronize them.

When milling big wood, I usually use a modified, 4-ft. Alaskan mill coupled to a Stihl 090 engine with a double-headed Cannon bar **(3)**. The Granberg Helper Handle, which is attached to the bar end, gives your partner something to hold on to.

170   CHAPTER 11   **Special Cuts**

1

2

3

Recently I have had great success with a Stihl 090G (gear drive) saw, especially on logs over 2 ft. in diameter. The only problem was the loss of gear oil from the venting hole in the top of the gear case cover with the saw in the milling position. So I removed the cotter pin and tapped the vent hole to accommodate a 90° elbow and a short piece of copper tube stuffed with a foam fuel-filter element. Without this modification, you have to check the level of gear oil constantly to guard against a ruined gear case.

The guide-plank/end-board system discussed on pp. 76-78 works well with any size log (**1,2,3**). Homemade, square-tube end dogs, bolted on with ⅜-in.-diameter lags (p. 54), secure the top slab here.

Although one-worker operations are possible, a team of two workers is best. With one worker on the winch and the other setting wedges, the mill is kept cutting and a day's production is greatly increased.

Plastic felling wedges are invaluable for moving heavy cants. This cant is over 10 in. thick, 3 ft. wide and 24 ft. long (**4**). The wedge in the foreground was driven in to help start the cant sliding as it pivoted on two wedges at the weight center.

1

2

3

4

You can hold one end of the cant in place with a small hatchet **(1)** while you position the other end for lifting. Then, to keep the cant from sliding, replace the hatchet with a lag bolt. Begin to lift with a jack positioned at the weight center of the log **(2)**. Use a block under the jack to increase its height. Wedge the cant with a block of wood **(3)** before you complete the lift, and position the log with a jack. The slabbed log makes an ideal working surface.

How to stabilize this mass of wood? Bolt the cant to a nearby log, stump or tree with a small log, using washered lag bolts.

For production milling, it's a good idea to have a smaller mill and bar as a companion to the 4-ft. mill. This 2-ft. Mark III **(4)** is modified for bolting to the bar, has standard thrust skids and a winching button. If you use the same saw engine for both mills, make sure to couple each new chain to a new sprocket to prolong the life of the chain.

During the milling, log ramps assist in the safe movement of slabs from the cant **(5,6)**.

1

2

3

4

5

6

Quartering a Log

If you want to mill very large trees, you will have to quarter the log first. Do this either by splitting the log with steel wedges and wooden gluts, or by freehand ripping with a chainsaw.

The drawing (1) shows how to split a log. To begin, mark vertical and horizontal index lines through the heart center of the butt of the log. If you find a major check, draw the vertical index line through it and make the split there. If no check exists, start one by sledge-hammering a checking or steel splitting wedge at the top of the vertical line so that it just starts to split the log. Remove the wedge and position it so that its top corner is guided by and connected to the first check. Hammer it in until the wood just starts to split, remove it and continue the process until you get to the bottom of the line. Leave the wedge in position at the bottom of the log for the next stage of splitting. These shallow checks will help the log split accurately along the line.

Now start a steel splitting wedge in the top of the check. Add other wedges at short distances below it. Pound each wedge in a short way, then go back and pound each in farther, repeating the process until all the wedges are driven home and the log begins to split. Complete the split using wooden gluts. Start the first glut into the split on the top of the log. Use more between the steel wedges. Drive the gluts in gradually until the wedges loosen.

As the top of the log begins to split, start gluts into the log's length. Double up on the gluts to complete the split. Repeat the process to quarter the halves. Use a chainsaw to cut binding splinters or redirect an offline split.

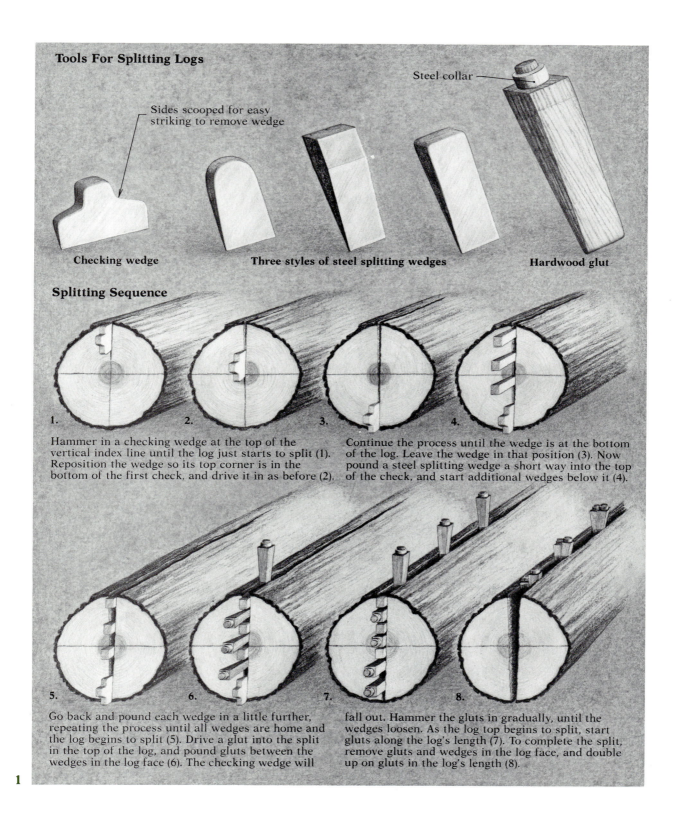

Tools For Splitting Logs

Steel collar

Sides scooped for easy striking to remove wedge

Checking wedge

Three styles of steel splitting wedges

Hardwood glut

Splitting Sequence

1.

2.

3.

4.

Hammer in a checking wedge at the top of the vertical index line until the log just starts to split (1). Reposition the wedge so its top corner is in the bottom of the first check, and drive it in as before (2).

Continue the process until the wedge is at the bottom of the log. Leave the wedge in that position (3). Now pound a steel splitting wedge a short way into the top of the check, and start additional wedges below it (4).

5.

6.

7.

8.

Go back and pound each wedge in a little further, repeating the process until all wedges are home and the log begins to split (5). Drive a glut into the split in the top of the log, and pound gluts between the wedges in the log face (6). The checking wedge will

fall out. Hammer the gluts in gradually, until the wedges loosen. As the log top begins to split, start gluts along the log's length (7). To complete the split, remove gluts and wedges in the log face, and double up on gluts in the log's length (8).

1

For milling, block up a quarter **(1)** with one split side level. Mount end boards and lag bolts to support the guide plank, and mill off the split side. Now roll the log so that the remaining split side is level, set the end boards square to the freshly milled surface and mill. Now you're ready to quartersaw or flatsaw the quarters.

On logs that don't split readily or accurately, or on logs that are curved or knotty, I use a chainsaw to cut down a chalked line running the length of the log between the tops of the vertical index lines. If the saw won't reach all the way through the log, you may have to roll it over to complete the cut, or use wedges and gluts to split the remaining wood.

This 52-ft. Sitka spruce log **(2)** was quartered, then quartersawn to be used in the box spar of a sailboat.

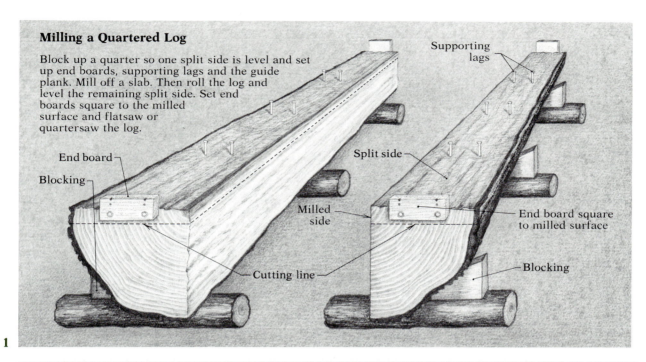

Milling a Quartered Log

Block up a quarter so one split side is level and set up end boards, supporting lags and the guide plank. Mill off a slab. Then roll the log and level the remaining split side. Set end boards square to the milled surface and flatsaw or quartersaw the log.

Supporting lags

End board

Blocking

Split side

Milled side

End board square to milled surface

Cutting line

Blocking

1

2

Chapter 12

Homemade Edger

There aren't many types of specialty mills on the market today, so I've designed a few that can be built in the home shop. The vertical edger is handy for cutting to depth, circle cutting and edging boards. Make it from two pieces of 3″ x 12″ channel iron and two pieces of 1½″ x 2″ flatstock iron bolted together (**3**).

The edger is mounted to an edging table (a slab of wood will do) that is nailed down securely (**1**). Center a short, straight line just a little longer than the width of your sawbar across the table for a sawbar slot (**2**). It's important to have ample room on both sides of the table to support the edger when it's mounted on the saw. Plunge-cut the slot with the nose of the bar (**4**). Then mount the edger, clamping the bar between the sandpapered mounts (**5**). Use the shortest bar you have that will handle the work. You can use either crosscutting or ripping chain, but for production milling, I recommend new modified ripping chain.

This setup is dangerous, so it's smart to use the adjustable, clamp-on safety guard shown in the drawing, even with a short bar. The guard is off in the following photos so you can see how the vertical edger is used.

1

2

Vertical Edger and Guard

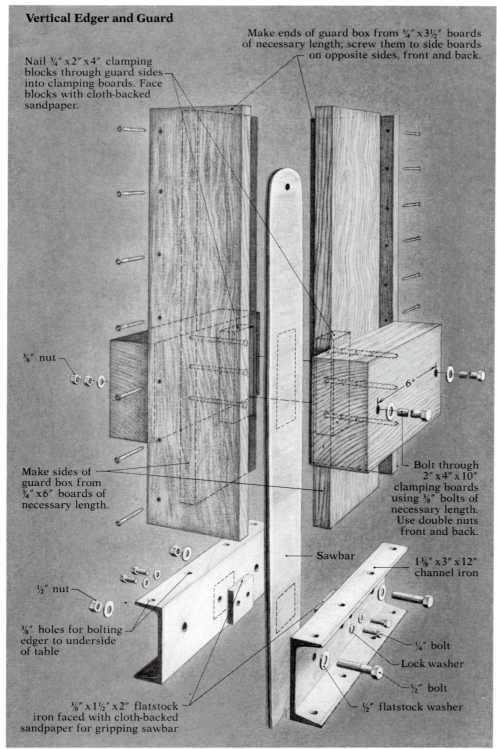

Make ends of guard box from ¾" x 3½" boards of necessary length; screw them to side boards on opposite sides, front and back.

Nail ¾" x 2" x 4" clamping blocks through guard sides into clamping boards. Face blocks with cloth-backed sandpaper.

⅜" nut

Make sides of guard box from ¾" x 6" boards of necessary length.

6"

Bolt through 2" x 4" x 10" clamping boards using ⅜" bolts of necessary length. Use double nuts front and back.

½" nut

⅜" holes for bolting edger to underside of table

Sawbar

1⅜" x 3" x 12" channel iron

¼" bolt

Lock washer

½" bolt

½" flatstock washer

⅜" x 1½" x 2" flatstock iron faced with cloth-backed sandpaper for gripping sawbar

3

4

5

181

Lower the bar into the slot **(1)** until the edger rests squarely on the table. Bolt the edger to the table using four ⅜-in. lags **(2)**.

Now mount the edger table to a stump with the sawbar up **(3)**, using four washered lag bolts. I use this system for small jobs, removing the table from the stump for refueling. (A tankful of fuel will cut several hundred feet of lumber.) You could also attach the edger table to sawhorses for portability and to eliminate the need to dismount the saw for refueling.

To edge quartersawn boards, first measure for desired board width **(4)**. Then, for a fence, position a dressed guide plank the distance of that measurement away from the sawbar. Measure from the inside edge of a chain cutter on both sides of the bar to make sure the fence is straight **(5)**. Clamp or nail down the fence securely **(6)**.

Start the engine with the throttle locked in the starting position. This half-open setting is adequate for edging most lumber. Or you can use the remote throttle attachment used in winch-milling.

Edge the boards **(7)**, readjusting the fence as necessary. For slabsawn boards, I mark a cutting line with chalk and remove the first edge freehand, then proceed using the fence.

1

2

3

4

5

6

7

183

Precision Depth Cuts

This is a good way to make some of the cuts necessary in timber joinery. Begin by marking the line of cut (**1**). Mount the edger so that the sawbar protrudes to the desired depth. Then measure the width of the edger (**2**), and center it on the cut line (**3**). Tack or clamp short guide boards along the marks (**4**). Enter the cut with the bottom of the edger level on the top of the timber (**5**), and exit the cut in the same way (**6**).

1

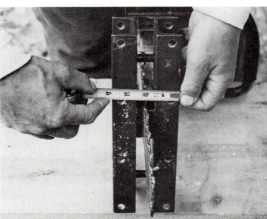

2

3

4

6

5

Cutting Circles

With the homemade edger, you can accurately cut circles in lumber of any thickness. The only limitation is the size of your sawbar. A new (or near-new) crosscut chain works best for cutting circles of small diameter. Don't use old chain—the set of a chain recedes with wear, which results in less clearance for the bar in the cut.

To begin, cut a board the length of a radius of the circle you wish to cut, plus extra for a handle. Mark a line across the board for the saw slot (**1**) and bore it out (**2**) (be careful of saw kick-back as you do this). Clamp the edger to the sawbar, insert the bar through the slot and bolt the unit to the board (**3**). Measure from the inside edge of a chain cutter and mark the desired radius in the center of the board (**4**). Drive a spike through the board at that mark for a pivot (**5**), and tack the spike into the center of the circle. Start the saw and enter the cut by pushing the handle end of the board (**6**).

1

2

3

4

5

6

Complete the cut (1) and remove the spike. By adjusting the depth of the sawbar and resetting the radii, you can cut curved dadoes.

An electric chainsaw works well indoors for massive cuts that would otherwise be difficult to make (2). One reason I designed this mill was to make a table big enough to sit at with a lot of my friends (3), a table that could be danced on when the time was right.

1

2

3

189

2x4 Mill

An accurate and inexpensive mill (1) can be built from a dressed 2x4, two feet of ½-in. threaded rod, four ½-in. flat washers, six ½-in. nuts, and a few scraps of 2x2s and plywood for spacers. Use several thicknesses of plywood, such as ¼ in., ⅜ in., ½ in., ⅝ in. and ¾ in., so you can set cutting height accurately.

Drill two ½-in. holes in the bar of your chainsaw for mounting. Lock together two of the nuts on the bottom ends of the threaded rods. Drill two ½-in. holes in the 2x4 guide rail, using the bar holes as a template. You can substitute a dressed 2x6 or a wider board for the 2x4 if you wish.

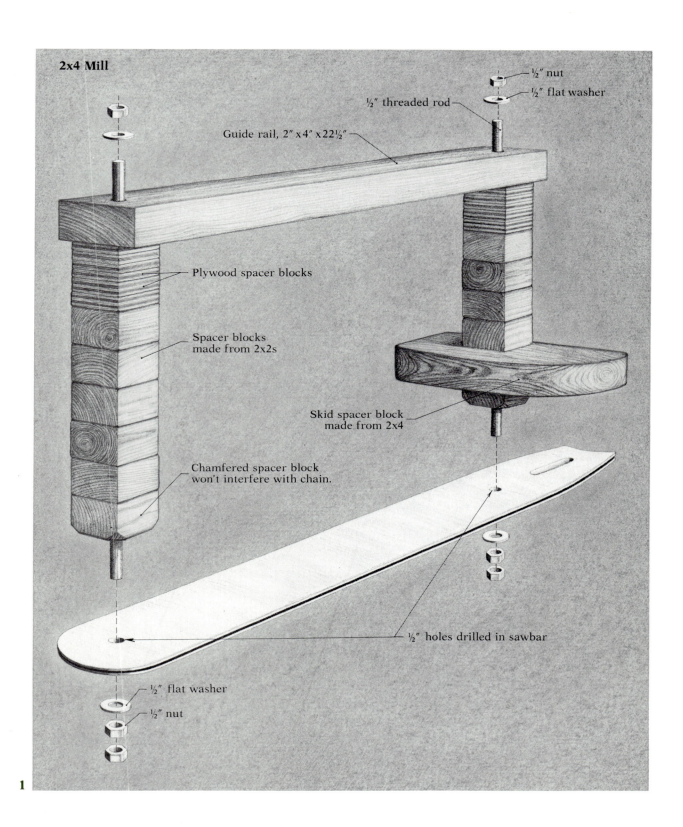

2x4 Mill

½" nut

½" flat washer

½" threaded rod

½" nut

½" flat washer

Guide rail, 2" x 4" x 22½"

Plywood spacer blocks

Spacer blocks made from 2x2s

Skid spacer block made from 2x4

Chamfered spacer block won't interfere with chain.

½" holes drilled in sawbar

½" flat washer

½" nut

1

To mill a square timber with the 2x4 mill, first set up the end boards and guide plank. Determine mill height by measuring from the top of the guide plank to where you want to make the first cut **(1)**. Assemble the mill with the necessary number of spacers, positioning the skid block below the bar with a regular block to keep the chain from pinching the skid. Stack surplus spacers above the guide rail **(2)** and secure the assembly with a flat washer and nut. Double-check cutting height by measuring from the edge of an inside tooth to the bottom of the guide rail **(3)**.

Mill through the first cut, as described on pp. 90-100 **(4)**. For the second cut, lay the guide plank back on top of the slab. Because the 2x4 mill has only one guide rail, you need to use the plank with every cut to control the mill during exit and entry. Reassemble the mill to adjust for your depth of cut, positioning the skid block above the bar with a regular spacer block in between **(5)** so that the skid will ride against the log during milling. The blocks next to the bar should be chamfered on one side so they can't interfere with the chain. Double-check mill height after torquing down the top nuts, then mill, using end dogs and kerf wedges **(6)**.

Now set the cant on edge and install the end boards **(1)**. Adjust the mill to the correct height and mill through the third cut, then the final cut **(2)**. Here is the completed timber **(3)**.

1

2

3

195

Mini-Mill

Mini-mills, which are available through many chainsaw dealers, work with the saw in a vertical position. To use one, you need a guide plank made from a straight board and the 4-ft. aluminum track sections that come with the mill (1). The mill does a reasonably good job of milling small logs, but I wouldn't recommend it for serious lumbermaking. It does do a nice job of edging (2) and, with an adjustable rip fence (3), is useful for ripsawing to width (4). A variety of freehand cuts (5) is also possible.

1

2

3

4

5

Angle Mill

I designed this mill to edge standard lumber, to mill angled lumber, and to make straight, angled and complex-angled precision depth cuts for timber joinery. You can make this mill from materials available from metal and machine-hardware supply houses **(1)**.

You'll need a hacksaw, a drill press with drills up to ½ in., a belt sander, ¼-in. and ⅜-in. taps, and an electric welder (though brazing can be substituted for welding if you prefer).

Angle Mill

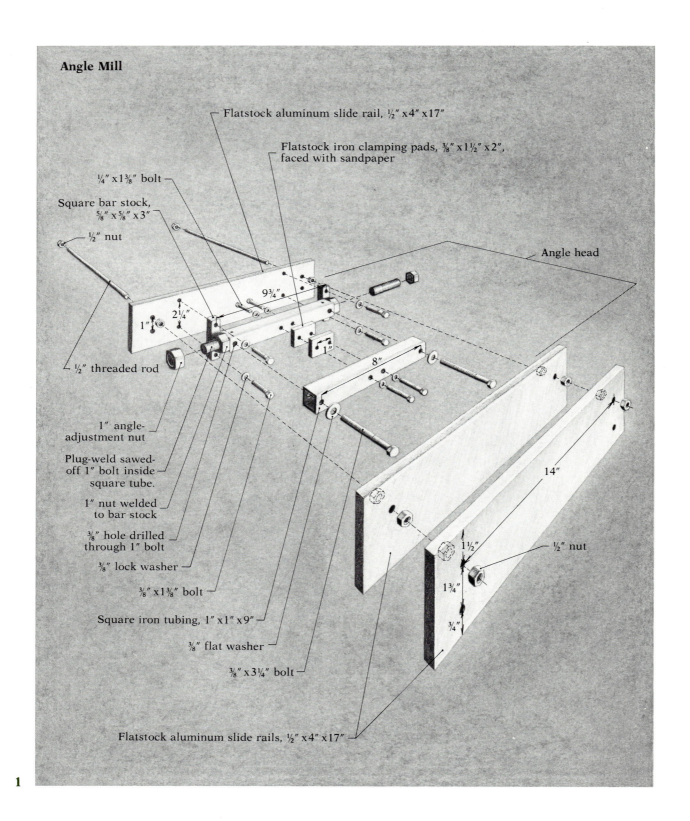

Flatstock aluminum slide rail, ½" x 4" x 17"

Flatstock iron clamping pads, ⅜" x 1½" x 2", faced with sandpaper

¼" x 1⅜" bolt

Square bar stock, ⅝" x ⅝" x 3"

½" nut

Angle head

9¾"

2¼"

1"

1"

8"

½" threaded rod

1" angle-adjustment nut

Plug-weld sawed-off 1" bolt inside square tube.

1" nut welded to bar stock

⅜" hole drilled through 1" bolt

⅜" lock washer

⅜" x 1⅜" bolt

Square iron tubing, 1" x 1" x 9"

⅜" flat washer

⅜" x 3¼" bolt

14"

1½"

1¾"

¾"

½" nut

Flatstock aluminum slide rails, ½" x 4" x 17"

1

To use the mill, mount the sawbar to the desired cutting depth, then cut two pieces of sandpaper twice the size of the clamping pads (1). Fold the pieces and insert them between the pads and the bar to hold the bar in place. Secure the bar by tightening the bolts evenly on the angle head, taking care not to overtighten (2). Tighten both angle-adjustment nuts (3) after positioning the bar to the angle you want. With this mill, a great number of inboard and outboard cutting positions are possible, as shown in the photographs (4,5,6).

1

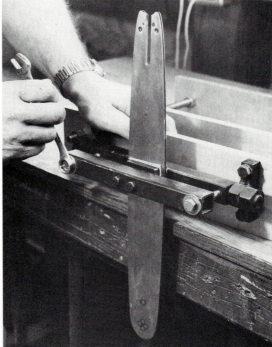

2

3

4

6

5

201

Timber Notches

The angle mill (1) lets you cut notches of all angles and depths from either side of a timber (2,3). When cutting the sides of the notch, the outside slide rail acts as a fence against the edge of the timber (4). Make sure the slide rails are always parallel to each other.

1

2

3

4

The last cut, which frees the notch wood, is made with the saw held vertically in the mill. Adjust the mill while holding one side of a square against the sawbar and the other side across the slide rails (1). Loosen the angle-head bolts with a wrench (2), adjust the saw to depth (3) and tighten the bolts. Mark the cut and the placement of the guide plank (4). Double-check the plank before nailing or clamping it in place (5).

1

2

CHAPTER 12   **Specialty Mills**

3

5

4

Mill carefully **(1)**, pushing the mill forward smoothly and steadily. Keep both hands away from the chain. Be sure that the bar is completely out of the cut and the chain is stopped before you lift the mill off the guide plank.

You can mill from both sides of the guide plank if you make it a width that is suitable for multiple cuts **(2)**. For cuts like these **(3)**, and for most timber joinery, I use standard crosscutting chain.

1

2

3

Chapter 13

Once you start to make your own lumber, you begin to notice usable wood everywhere you go. For example, I found these logs **(1)** washed up on a beach in the middle of a large city. I know a man who built most of his house from discarded powerline poles, which yielded beautiful, dry fir and cedar boards. Don't overlook existing timbers and beams either— resawing them often yields surprising results. You're not restricted to milling only standing trees.

If you mill your own wood, you're not limited to working with the sizes and species available at the lumberyard. Gilbert Cook, of Alert Bay, B.C., makes sure he gets attractive grain patterns for his mandolins **(2)** by milling the spruce, maple and rosewood himself. (Using my system, Cook is also rebuilding a 65-ft. boat with milled lumber.) And although oversized timbers such as these **(3)** can be difficult to find commercially, they are easy to make with a chainsaw.

1

2

Albert Myshrall

3

209

Epilogue

This sailboat was built entirely from milled wood (1). Milled cedar works well as decking and skirting for this hot tub (2), which in turn works well for fishing.

Master gunstock maker Byrd Pearson (3), of Provo, Utah, relies on wood with fine crotch grain for his gunstock blanks. Lumberers such as Scot Wineland (4, center) of Chico, Calif., are able to provide these special cuts using chainsaw-lumbermaking techniques. This piece of Claro walnut is only one example.

Dale Nish (5), of Provo, Utah, turns his bowls from milled local woods that are almost impossible to buy: chestnut, apple, cottonwood and apricot, to name just a few.

1

2

3

4

5

The Haida Indian Band Museum **(1)**, in Skidegate, B.C., is housed in a building constructed totally of milled wood. George Dyson, of Ioco, B.C., planked the inside of his baidarka, *The Mount Fairweather*, with 40-ft. Sitka spruce that he milled himself **(2)**. It's incredible to look at, on and off the water **(3)**. And Alfie Collinson, also of Skidegate, B.C., uses milled yellow cedar slabs as the raw material for his sculptures **(4)**.

With a chainsaw, a few tools and imagination, the possibilities of lumbermaking are endless. What more can I say?

1

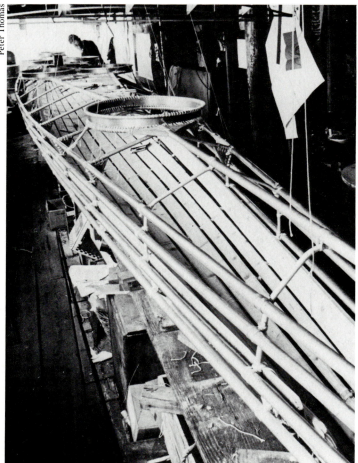

2

3

4

Editor: Laura Cehanowicz Tringali

Designer: Roger Barnes

Layout, Illustration, Cover Design: Lee Hochgraf Hov

Consultant: John Kelsey

Editorial Assistant: Deborah Cannarella

Manager of Production Services: Cindy Lee Nyitray

Production Coordinator: Mary Galpin

Typesetting: Nancy-Lou Knapp

Pasteup: Jean Zalkind Anderheggen,
Claudia Westerbeke Chapman,
Johnette Luxeder, Karen Pease

Typeface: Compugraphic Aster 10 point

Printer: R.R. Donnelley & Sons Co., Chicago, Ill.

Paper: Warren Patina, 70 lb., Neutral pH

AU